EXPERIENCES:
*Life at a Continuing Care
Retirement Community*

EXPERIENCES:

Life at a Continuing Care Retirement Community

by Residents of Kendal at Longwood

Peggy & Allan Brick, Editors

EXPERIENCES, Kendal at Longwood,
201 Kendal Drive, Kennett Square PA 19348

Printed in the USA by McNaughton-Gunn

Book and Cover Design by Fran Nimeck
Cover photos courtesy of Norm Ganser, Karen Halstead,
Fran Nimeck, Pat Redmond, Sarah Zimmerman

ISBN: 978-0-692-44578-5
www.Kendal.org, www.KCC.Kendal.org,
www.KCArboretum.org

Contents

Our Outdoors

Favorite Places

Creative Lives

It Happened Right Here!

Our Caring Community

Introduction
Peggy Brick

"There are no good books about CCRCs!" our new neighbor declared. We were having dinner with Bob and Betty Warner, indulging in a discussion of our wisdom in having moved to Kendal, a Continuing Care Retirement Community. We were sharing stories of aging friends who, in spite of their unpredictable futures, seemed not to understand the independence and security they could have living in a Continuing Care Retirement Community. Immediately, we knew it was time to create a book in which residents would tell stories about their lives in this vigorous community, Kendal at Longwood. People needed to know!

Over forty years ago, a small group of Quakers recognized the need for a new way of living as people age. They envisioned a community where people first live independently in cottages, but as they need further support move to a Health Center where they receive additional care as needed. The Kendal motto, "Together, Transforming the Experience of Aging," expresses the belief that life in a community provides unique opportunities for growth and creativity as well as safety as people age.

For those of us living here at Kendal, this becomes a very special time of life. Relieved of many earlier responsibilities, supported by a competent and caring staff, we have time to explore new ways of being. In the poignant memoir *Let Evening Come*, 89 year-old resident Mary Morrison identified the way to judge a good retirement home: "Wheelchairs are allowed in the dining room and there's no activity director." Amazingly simple but profound criteria. As revealed in several of our stories, when people become disabled, either physically or cognitively, they are not segregated but remain part of a caring community. They are welcomed not only in the dining room but they are brought to events—films, concerts, forums, meetings—by staff and by other residents.

When a visitor asked me, "What do you like best about Kendal?" I hesitated. After living here for eleven years, I could identify more and more reasons, but finally I replied, "There's a role for everyone." While an excellent staff provides activities for residents in Personal Care (Assisted Living) and the Nursing area, residents who live independently create a bounty of activities that are the foundation of community life. A few choose not to take an active part, and their choice is respected. However, most of us discover a rich variety of ways to participate. If something is missing or needs improving, we join a committee or start one. For example, recently a team of new residents identified the need to coordinate the plethora of information being distributed and created a Communications Committee that developed a comprehensive website that reports news of all community activities as well as contributions from over 70 committees.

It was in the Kendal spirit of responding to a problem with, "So what are you going to do about it?" that we invited residents to "Help Us Write a Book—about LIFE AT KENDAL" The stories were to be "an experience that shows that this is a community where people can fulfill themselves in what for many is the most valuable time in their lives." As a result, this book is a crazy combination of the responses, some funny, some profound, some poignant, some powerful— a delightful potpourri, each piece a revelation of life here.

Of course, the book is in no way a comprehensive description of life at Kendal. Some of our most treasured events are missing: the bi-weekly concerts; Monday Topics, bringing speakers on a wide variety of contemporary issues;films,both contemporary and documentary;the wood-shop, where residents repair almost anything; the pottery room where professional potters and new explorers meet; book groups and photographers' programs enabling arm-chair travel; and the abundance of wellness classes, where we challenge our growing diminishments.

Yes, the opportunities are endless and for each of us they keep changing. Some of the activities we enjoyed when we arrived a youthful 75, are not possible today. So what's possible at 86? Why, we could recruit our friends and neigh-bors to share their experiences of living at Kendal! Together, we could create a book to help people understand why, day by day, we love our life in this community. This is it!

Why Kendal?

In that perfect moment of joy and camaraderie, Merritt began singing the beautiful, sacred and well-known round "Dona Nobis Pacem." With great glee, this crowd of celebrating singers touched the walls with their voices and thrilled at the reverberations.

— BOB AND BETTY WARNER

It Takes a Lot of Courage
Marilyn Van Savage

It takes a lot of courage to admit to yourself that you're getting old. I came to that conclusion about ten years ago when I looked in the mirror and saw staring back at me a face I didn't want to admit was mine. That woman looking at me had laugh lines that were there even though she definitely wasn't laughing and a body that was obviously not perky any longer. Deterioration had set in and I couldn't avoid it.

I was sharing my feeling of remorse regarding this situation with my good friend, Gloria, when she commented on something she had been thinking. "I think it's time we go into a retirement home."

"You mean an old folks home?" I screeched indignantly.

"No, just wait a minute," she said. "We don't have to look at it that way, just a nice place to spend the rest of our lives."

Well, I finally calmed down and gave it some thought. Maybe it would be good to go someplace with other people our own age; some place where I wouldn't have to think about climbing the stairs to my bedroom, mowing the lawn or driving to doctor appointments. Thus started a period of exploration: looking at "retirement homes" not too far from northern Delaware.

We looked and we looked: places that looked like institutions, places that were high rise, and places with no nursing facilities. We were feeling discouraged. Then, finally, we saw

Kendal at Longwood. I fell in love with the grounds as soon as I drove down the lane. Magnificent trees lined the walkways–and speaking of walkways, how wonderful it was that they were covered! The apartments being at ground level was a definite plus. And the nursing care section had a feature that I knew I would appreciate in the future–private rooms. That meant that I would not have to share a room with some old, cranky senile person since I was not planning on being senile myself, or cranky for that matter!

Then it was settled, we were coming to Kendal. We had each chosen a one bedroom-apartment. Finally, after a two year wait Gloria moved in, and then it was my turn six weeks later. Our trip into the last part of our life had begun.

Now, over eight years later, I have to admit I'm not getting old. I am old. And what has Kendal been like? Well, for me it's great. The people on the staff are wonderful. The other residents are friendly and even though I am not a Quaker, I appreciate their values. But I'd have to say that most of all, I love what I first saw when I drove into Kendal, the beautiful grounds.

I especially appreciate their beauty if I'm feeling a little blue. Some mornings I just don't want to get out of bed, but then my dog, Christie, sits staring at me and I know she's sending me a message: "Hey, get up Mom, it's time to take a walk." So I dress, get her leash and walk out the door. At Kendal it doesn't matter what the weather is; even if it's raining or snowing, I can walk clear to the end of the grounds without getting wet by staying on the sidewalk under the covered walkways. As I follow the sidewalk past the apartments, I admire the flowers people have planted by their door.

As I walk around the grounds, Christie stops along the way to check if any of her doggie friends have left messages in the surrounding grass. My neighbor tells me her dog leaves us a "pee-mail" near our door early each morning.

Having a dog here at Kendal is a great socializing tool; I'm sure many people stop and talk to me just so they can pet Christie and tell me about some wonderful dog they have known.

Christie is especially delighted when she sees one of her people friends who stoop to pet and talk to her. She goes into a frenzy, wagging her tail, giving a yelp of delight when she meets a special woman from the Housekeeping staff whom we meet as she is getting ready to go into a resident's apartment to clean. Christie knows this special friend will give her a treat. When we see her in the distance, I let go of Christie's leash and she streaks over the sidewalk to greet her. She asks Christie to sit, gives her the treat and a hug. Christie gives her a kiss in return. It is a special encounter we look forward to every morning.

Other days, when the weather is especially nice, we head out around the perimeter path. Then I can really see the beauty of the grounds. As I walk down the path, the sun filters through the leaves and branches of the tall trees. Often I see a variety of living creatures along the way: squirrels chasing each other down the path and up a tree, rabbits hopping by the side of the road and sometimes even deer peeking out between the tree trunks.

So, even though I have started the eighth decade of my life and can no longer deny that I am old, being here at Kendal helps me forget that fact. The beauty of this place takes my breath away and makes me realize something: this is one of the happiest times of my life. I just step out my door and look. I am grateful.

Moving Day

Douglas Spencer

The barn will be the last stop on our goodbye visit. Just an hour ago we signed the papers to complete the sale of our house in the country. We go to the barn for the last time. It has no residents now. No whinnies are heard as we approach the stalls. Ever since Janet was a little girl she had wanted to have a horse. Ten years ago we got our first ones, and she said that she had just made her goal of getting a horse by the time she was sixty-five. Now, in preparation for our move to a retirement community 100 miles away, we had found other accommodations for our two horses. But there is still the smell of hay in the hay room and of fresh wood shavings in the stalls. We savor the view across the paddock and the fields, the memories of watching the barn being built, of having our first horses brought to us from "Lost and Found Horse Rescue" in York, of taking care of those beautiful, powerful but kind animals...it is all there, and we will miss it.

"I sure hope we're doing the right thing," Janet says.

"I know," I say. "I get those same doubts too. But we can't stay here in the country forever."

We have had this cliché-laced conversation many times in the last six months. This time we are having it as we pack up the last of our belongings before getting in our two cars and heading for that retirement community we now will call home.

The two hour trip from Carlisle to Kennett Square goes uneventfully.

We park our vehicles as close to the apartment as we can, lead our patient dog Kerri on a leash and carry in her dog bed. This time when we enter our apartment it is no longer "that place we are moving to," but "our new home." We put Kerri's bed in a nice corner where she can see everything that is going on and we tell her this is where we are going to live now. She seems to know, even as we go in and out, that we will be here. Kitty Boy and Kitty Girl are glad to see their kitty litter box after a two hour trip in their cages.

We look around at our empty rooms.

"Wow," Janet says. "They did a wonderful job of painting the walls. That one darker wall really does look nice."

"Well, of course," I say with a smile, "You chose the colors."

That was the deal. We had our choice of colors. If we wanted anything other than Kendal's standard colors, we would buy the paint and the Kendal staff would do the painting.

We look out the back window at the view across the field to the woods. That view was what had really sold us on this apartment, and we are not disappointed today. The "office" that had been a walk-in closet has the window that we had asked for, and a built-in counter where we will put our computer. I can see that I will need to make a few shelves for this nook.

On one of our trips to unload the Honda we are greeted by Peggy Brick. She reminds us (although we didn't need reminding) that we had met her four months ago when we were here for our day of interviews. We remember that encounter well. We were in the coffee shop taking a lunch break between our late morning and early afternoon appointments, when a person came up, introduced herself and said, "You look like you are new here. How is it going?"

We had chatted and she told us about her program of

discussions called "Transitions" which helps newcomers adjust to the newness of living in this community, and she assured us that in spite of the effort involved in moving, we would like it here. Now here we are, truly new people and here is Peggy again, welcoming us.

The movers arrive, and we dig into unpacking. Soon we have filled an empty box with packing materials and Janet goes out to put it in the trash and recycling bins which we understand are near our parking lot.

She returns a few minutes later.

"Well," she says, "I just met one of our neighbors. His name is Cooey, and he helped me find the trash and recycling room. He says we are a little late to enjoy the tomatoes from his garden, but I found out how we can have a garden next year. The gardens are down by the tennis court."

We had a garden in Carlisle, in fact two…a vegetable garden and a flower garden, and her gardens are one of the things Janet is particularly sad about leaving.

We get back to work, and by six o'clock we have enough unpacked so that we feel we can take a break and have dinner. At the entrance to the dining room we are greeted by a hostess who recognizes us as new, and asks if we would like to start a table, eat by ourselves, or join the Smiths, who just came in.

"We don't know the Smiths" we reply, "But that would be fine if it is ok with them."

"I'm sure it is," the hostess says, "And I'm Millie. I know you are the Spencers because of your meal card, and I'll introduce you to them."

Millie leads us to a table for 6 and does the introductions. We discover that George and Marjorie Smith live just around the corner from us, and have been here for 5 years. We are barely into our conversation when Millie arrives with another couple.

"The Walshes would like to join you," she says.

Now our table for six is filled. The Walshes moved here from nearby West Chester. Dave had been a physics professor. His wife, Mary was a stay-at-home mom.

So we have a very friendly and welcoming table, and they all reassure us about how happy they are to be here, and how much we will find here to keep us busy. In fact, they warn, don't sign up for everything right away.

The next morning, Saturday, our son Tom arrives from his home about an hour away in the northern Philadelphia suburbs. Although he had been with us for one of the pre-moving seminars that Kendal holds for prospective residents, this is the first he has seen of our choice of apartment.

"You really have a wonderful view!" Tom says. "And it looks like everything is going to fit ok. You must have gotten rid of tons of stuff."

"Yes," I reply. "We did get rid of those shelves of old jelly glasses. How are you coming with that project?"

It is an in-joke, because it was at the Preparing for Moving seminar we all attended together when that bit of advice was given. Tom had given an exaggerated startle and said that he'd better start now.

The doorbell rings. It is a member of the resident "Welcoming Committee" just stopping in to say hello, and to ask when would be a good time to stop back to answer any questions we might have about such things as where the grocery stores are. She gives us a thick loose-leaf notebook that includes a directory of all Kendal residents, lists of committees, lists of staff, and on and on.

"More than you want to know, I'm sure," she says, "But look through it at your leisure and call me any time you have a question. And on Monday, we'd love it if you could join several of us for dinner."

Janet and I exchange sure-why-not looks.

"Thank you very much," we reply. "We'd love to."

She writes down her name and phone number and shows us how to find her apartment.

We go back to putting books on shelves and taking the few remaining things in from our car. We have lunch from sandwich makings we had brought from Carlisle, and then all three of us make a trip to the center to see if we have any mail in our new mail box.

"I don't see how you are ever going to get anything done around here," Tom says after that trip. "Every time we go somewhere someone stops you and says, 'You must be the Spencers. Welcome,' and then there's all this where are you from, and we are sure you will like it here, and what are you interested in talk."

He is right, of course. We have met so many people in the barely 24 hours we have been here. After the second "You must be the Spencers" we asked how they knew.

"Your name is on channel 9, our in-house TV Channel," was the reply.

We hadn't hooked up our TV yet, so didn't realize that Channel 9 has a daily listing of activities, meal menus, and "Please welcome our new residents...." with the names and apartment number of people who just moved here.

We do more unpacking and putting things away, and by midafternoon Tom says he has to go back home, but is delighted with how we are settling in so well.

Over the next few weeks we gradually lose some, but not all of that feeling of being overwhelmed. We are invited to get involved in many groups and choose a few.

On Thanksgiving, just two months after we moved in, we play host to 14 family members. Millie had said it would be no trouble to set one very long table in the dining room, and we and discover how easy it is to have a Thanksgiving gathering when someone else (Kendal dining service) is doing the cooking and cleaning up. Our two sons and their families express their sincere appreciation that we are taking care of ourselves, and they all go home assured that Mom and Dad are not wilting away in some "old folks home."

At Christmas time our daughter and her husband come down from New Hampshire for a visit. Sue, her husband, Doug, and their two dogs all manage to sleep in our second bedroom, for which Kendal has temporarily supplied a second fold-out cot.

At breakfast after their first night here, Sue says, "We all really appreciate how you guys have planned ahead, and are taking care of yourselves. But you must still miss Carlisle and the horses and all."

"Yes," we both admit.

"I'm finally beginning to get over it," Janet says, "I still seem to spend lots of time just sitting and knitting. But we are getting more involved here."

We tell Sue some of the things we are doing...being on one of the entertainment committees, participating in the Kendal chorus, the political activities leading up to the election last month, the shelves I made in the woodshop, the regular exercise group in the Kendal gym, Tuesday evening bridge.

"Good grief!" Sue says. "I'd say you'd better watch out that you don't take on *too much*! It seems to me that you have more than settled in."

We think about it, and not just for the first time. Yes, we do miss our old home and all it represented. It has been a flurry of activity since that September moving day. We have left a home, but here we have found a community. We will be okay. In fact we think we will do well.

And indeed we have.

Putting Down Roots
Lark Worth

The first time I talked seriously to my husband, Fernando, about moving to Kendal was from a hospital bed in intensive care. I had entered the hospital for a routine ablation surgery for my heart, only to end up with life threatening complications that I was lucky to live through.

Of course, Fernando thought I was just under the influence of the pain medication and humored me, but deep in my heart I knew that I would not be able to care for him in our current home as he was already dealing with serious health issues. He is 18 years my senior and had signed us up for Kendal when he turned 65. I don't think he truly thought he would ever go, but he realized it was a good insurance policy...just in case.

As my health and energy returned, I persisted and we even came to an open house at Kendal. However, Fernando became increasingly nervous that I was serious and he steadfastly refused to go. I was under age and could not go without him—not that I would. So, after announcing firmly that when I turn 65 we would go, I put my new found energy elsewhere.

For the first time in my adult life, I started a vegetable garden. I had loved gardening with my parents growing up but as an adult always seemed to have more pressing commitments. Then 10 years earlier, I was diagnosed with fibromyalgia, a condition that creates chronic pain and fatigue with repetitive movements. Gardening, particularly weeding, was out of the question as I looked longingly from my home to where I could have put a garden.

But now, the surgery had given me a new lease on life. Many years before I had read about Square Foot Gardening in raised beds and thought this might work for me. With my husband's and nephew's help, I build a series of cedar raised beds including a pyramid shaped one for strawberries and one that was 4' x 8' on a table top. I was ecstatic to see the lettuces, peppers, carrots, tomatoes, cucumbers, zucchini, and of course strawberries thrive.

I also put my energy into forming a new interfaith organization called ACT in Faith of Greater West Chester to help our neighbors meet their basic needs in the midst of the Great Recession. A year later, when I was knee-deep in a major fundraiser, we received a call from Mike in the Admissions Department at Kendal for his yearly check-in. While I was telling him we would need to wait another two years until I turn 65, my Fernando interrupted the conversation.

Much to my surprise, he was changing his mind. But now, I wasn't ready to go! I had the major fundraiser coming up and of course my garden. I was finally putting down roots and wasn't ready to go.

Following a lot heart-to-heart soul searching, we agreed to meet with Mike. Much to his surprise, we were ready to commit that first meeting. We saw an apartment that would work just right for us and agreed to move within four months to get a special discount offer. The decision felt right, but there remained lots of emotions. Surprisingly one of the hardest ones for me was giving up my garden. It had brought such joy and comfort. I knew I wouldn't be able to grow vegetables at our new apartment, as its one drawback was that it was enveloped in shade year round.

I feared that I would not be allowed to have raised beds in the community garden. So, it was with much trepidation that I called Althea, the chair of the Committee, even before we moved. I would learn later what heart of gold she had, but she has a very brisk manner when we first talked and I was a bit intimidated. When I finally got through explaining my hope to have raised beds in the community garden, my heart did truly leap for joy as she said, "Sure, shouldn't be a problem. I just put in the first 4' high raised bed myself so I can't imagine anyone would complain." And they didn't!

My beds were right next to Althea's. I was still a bit intimidated by her. She had a booming voice and everyone knew just what was on her mind. After painstakingly installing a rack for my hose, she boomed: "Lark, you are going to have to raise that rack so I can weed whack under it." When my friends helped me install my strawberry pyramid and table top raised bed just like the ones I had left behind, she sat at her garden and watched like a hawk. I don't know what she thought might happen, or if she was just curious. Another time she called me at 7:30 one evening to find out if I had taken her first watermelon of the season. (We never did find out what happened to that watermelon.) Yet, we had a growing respect for each other. She had such a love for the garden. Her energy and enthusiasm for nurturing life, both the vegetables and the gardeners, was contagious.

Late that summer she stopped by my apartment with four bags of watermelon to give to the folks at ACT in Faith. We sat and talked a long time. Nothing special: just what was happening in the garden and how important it was for our families to have some wholesome food. I couldn't believe when I learned later that on that very afternoon, she had a massive heart attack and never recovered. All of us in the community garden were in shock. It took two co-chairs to replace her! Yet Althea's legacy lives on among us, each in our own way. There is a profound love and respect for the garden and for each other, and it shows. This summer our gardens are in full bloom. Twice a week I take bags of lettuce, cucumbers, tomatoes, zucchini, beans, carrots, and yes even some strawberries donated by fellow gardeners to ACT in Faith. The sense of joy this brings cannot be put in words, yet in my heart I know my roots are now firmly planted in my new home.

Two Generations
at Kendal / Crosslands
M. "Cal" Calvache

"Are you going home to Philadelphia?" my seatmate asked on returning from the restroom on our Friday afternoon flight from Denver.

"No," I said. "I live near West Chester."

"Oh, we just moved to Kennett Square," she responded.

The nice elderly woman clearly wanted the conversation to continue. "Where in Kennett Square?" I asked.

"Kendal, it's a Continuing Care Retirement Community on Baltimore Pike near Longwood Gardens."

My mother and stepfather lived three hours away and I made the roundtrip weekly to help with maintenance. My attention piqued, I said, "My neighbor's daughters work in the dining room. It's not a nursing home?"

She faced me and said, "Oh no, it's much more than that. We have an excellent nursing care facility and an assisted living section but most residents live independently. Kendal encourages independence and provides all the support facilities and services we need. My husband was a surgeon in Cleveland. As retirement approached, he researched CCRCs across the country, especially their medical facilities, and described Kendal as the best. He put us on the waiting list at four of the Kendals, each near one of our kids. Kendal at Longwood was the first to offer us a cottage, so we sold our house and moved as quickly as we could. It's wonderful; we couldn't be happier."

As she and I continued chatting, I became more and more convinced Mom and my step-father, Tom, should visit. Saturday morning, my wife and I called Mom and invited them to spend the next weekend with us so we could visit Kendal that Monday. Their response was cool to the idea, as Tom had become stubbornly independent and they lived in the house Mom and my late father built in 1939. The prospect of change is hard as we age but they agreed to look. I called Kendal to make the appointment.

We arrived to a warm welcome. A tour of the main building and a nice cottage followed. We returned to Admissions to discuss Kendal's acceptance requirements and financial issues. After providing documentation and disclosures, we were asked, "Do you have any questions?"

Tom, formerly a Chase Manhattan vice president, said, "Just one: do I understand that we will be investing a signi ficant amount of money for a residence which will never be included in our net worth, and we pay rent besides?"

"Not really," said the woman and quickly added, "The entrance fee is not for the purchase of a residence. Kendal owns it and maintains it at no cost to you. The fee is a down payment on guaranteed lifetime care and a significant part of that entrance fee is deductible as a medical expense on your income tax. The "rent" as you describe it covers one meal a day, all maintenance, housekeeping, utilities except telephone, and medical care.

Tom nodded, stood, extended his hand and said, "Thank you for the tour. This is a very impressive setup. And you've given us a lot to think about."

Mom didn't say anything beyond repeating Tom's thanks. As we left I allowed Mom and Tom to get a little ahead, turned to our hostess, shrugged, and said, "Thank you. I am impressed, I'll work on them."

With a smile she said, "Thank you and don't think anything of it. That reaction is not unusual."

Mom, Tom, and I got into the car and as we drove off, Tom said, "That's the worst investment I ever heard of."

I said, "Tom, the investment is in lifetime care that includes a place to live. The investment is in the care, not the real estate."

His response was, "Yeah, well, health care isn't valued in my estate."

In later discussions with Mom, it became clear that she liked the prospect of moving to Kendal but knew Tom would never go along. She did, however, send Kendal the fee putting them on the waiting list—as it turned out, a smart move. A few years later Tom died, after which Mom called Kendal and indicated a one-bedroom would suit her needs, which moved her up on the waiting list.

Shortly thereafter, Crosslands had a second floor apartment available and asked if she would like to see it. Mom asked, "Is there a covered walkway all the way to the main building?"

"Yes, it's in Brinton, the building closest to the center."

Long story short, Mom entered Crosslands in October of 1998. She made new friends; enjoyed living only a few miles from me, her only son, and all the conveniences that offered; and with no need to shop, she gave up driving rather than get a Pennsylvania driver's license. She took part in musical and other activities; and on reflection probably said to herself many times, "I made a good decision to come here. I am receiving much better care than if I had counted on Cal to take care of me. He loves me but is not a patient care giver." A correct assessment.

Observing your mother successfully undertake a major move and lifestyle change based on your recommendation is a relief. Not that there was any doubt, but still... .

In November, after my neurosurgeon relieved arthritic pressure on my spinal cord, he suggested the need for rehabilitation and that I not immediately return to my two-story home where I then lived alone. A Bryn Mawr Rehabilitation Hospital doctor came to my Paoli Hospital room and determined, "You do not qualify for in-patient status because you can use the bathroom unassisted." Kendal was suggested as an alternative. My surgeon, clearly annoyed by Bryn Mawr's assessment, had other patients rehabilitate here and wholeheartedly approved. Since my retirement plans included Kendal, I thought, "What a great opportunity to check it out."

So, on Medicare's tab, the "checking out" began. A very pleasant Social Services person welcomed me to Westmorland, told me how things worked, and got my signature on many forms. I didn't pay a lot of attention. I figured my surgeon was more than pleased and Mom's experience had been good.

The parade of nurses wearing nametags began. The first nurse introduced herself and said, "I'm here to take your blood pressure and blood ox." She did and said, "Great." Seeing the wheelchair and walker, she asked, "Can you get in and out of bed by yourself? How mobile are you?"

"Yes, I can get in and out of bed, to the chair, and to the bathroom with the walker. I'll sit in the wheelchair to brush my teeth and shave. Do you guys do this blood pressure thing every day?"

Smiling, she said, "Every shift."

I asked the 2nd shift nurse, "When does your shift end?"

"Eleven," she answered. "Why?"

I said, "Well, the hospital nurses awakened me in the middle of the night to go through this routine and then I couldn't go back to sleep. I made a deal with the night nurse to schedule me so that didn't happen. Can you guys do the same thing? I'm an early riser so, if I'm last on the list for midnight shift, I'll probably already be awake."

"I don't see why we can't work something out. I'll ask." She responded with a smile.

Sure enough, before six o'clock the next morning, as I

lay in bed, already awake; my room suddenly came alive. A cheery "Good morning," accompanied the lights. A quick meet and greet preceded the blood reading routine. That over with, I dressed, performed my morning ablutions, and turned on the TV to the business news while awaiting delivery of the breakfast ordered the day before. Belgian waffles with all the trimmings arrived shortly and I thought, "I could get used to this!"

A woman entered the room the next day, introduced herself, and asked, "Will you need laundry service?"

"Yes, that would be great," I said.

"Just put your dirty clothes in this bag. I'll pick them up once a week and return clean clothes, usually the next day. I'll hang ironed shirts in your closet."

"Wow! This is better than a wife," I thought.

Volunteers dropped by to refresh my water pitcher, offer snacks, and chat.

Anticipating boredom, I had packed a deck of cards. For years I'd played solitaire on my computer but now found, much to my despair, I couldn't shuffle the cards. Apparently, the nerve damage not only affected my left leg. "This is unacceptable! I've got to figure out how to do this!"

Little by little, my left hand began to respond to mental commands and awkward shuffles followed. I played solitaire and watched TV for two hours after breakfast everyday. The informal P.T. soon worked.

The scrolling CNBC market ticker occupied much of the day. As stock prices fell during the beginning of the "Great Recession," I looked for buying opportunities.

Nurses stopped in but often didn't do anything medically. I began to wonder why. Recalling stories abut nurse/patient relationships, my ego wondered, "Are they 'chatting me up?'" After all, I was by far the youngest patient and aside from limited mobility, was healthy and single. One day I mentioned, "I'm on the Kendal waiting list."

"Be careful when you get here," came the warning.

"Why?" I asked.

"There are a lot more single women than men," she said with a smile.

"My mother told me the same thing," I replied, and added, "Look, I'm twice divorced and obviously not good at it so I'm not going to do it again."

"Well, how long were you married?" she asked. Her continued interest struck me as curious—maybe single female residents were not the only threat.

"Total, about 32 years. They must have kept me around for some reason, right?"

"Well, if you ask me, you picked the wrong women." She said with a smile. I later learned her postgraduate major was psychology and a career change to marriage counseling a possibility. I was a lab project; she was not a threat. Reality set in and her declaration became food for thought and softened the blow to my ego. I realized my room had become the unofficial "break room." Nurses had found a place to relax between call bells. They checked on me, confirming nothing wrong, otherwise not interested. "Oh well... ."

After 30 days, Social Services informed me that Medicare would no longer cover Kendal's services and that I would move to Cumberland where per diem charges became my responsibility. I'd have my own shower, an improvement, but I'd have to navigate my wheelchair to the Coffee Shop for meals and to the nursing station for meds; and there was no cable! I had become spoiled in Westmorland. Life in Cumberland was good but only lasted a week. After all, the expenses of maintaining a large house continued and added to Cumberland fees...I'd figure out how to go up and down stairs and otherwise get along.

Mom's experience added to my own made the decision to enter Kendal in February of 2012 a "no brainer." Surgery in 2008 left me with a mobility issue but the day I moved in, a local vendor delivered my electric cart. That and a walker give me safe access to all the activities and services Kendal offers. Living here exceeded my expectations. The group of second-generation Kendal/Crosslands residents continues to grow as children realize the benefits of unburdening their own children from parental care.

In February 2014, my mother, Olive V. Calvache, passed away comfortably at the age of 96. In my opinion, she owed much of her longevity to good care and the low stress environment. As the end approached, she received wonderful, compassionate attention from the staff.

I'm blessed; Kendal is wonderful.

Marianne Had the Best Ideas
Peter Schindler

Marianne and I signed up for Kendal years before we actually came. Our children were 'lifers' at Westtown School. Marianne taught pottery there for 16 years, and I was the consulting psychiatrist for even longer. Kendal was the name everyone knew and the place to be when retirement beckoned.

Our new contemporary house on Denton Hollow Road designed by us and a local architect, was ready to move in. However, Marianne had been concerned about abdominal complaints although her generalist gave no undue cause for alarm. Then the OB/GYN became alarmed, evaluation and surgery followed and late stage ovarian cancer was diagnosed, with as much of it removed as possible.

During ten years of chemo, hair loss, and consultation, Marianne and I shared life even more closely. Our new home was a joy, totally different from the one we left in our valley. Marianne knew and lived the decline which I would not see—could not—let myself see.

In November, 2008 we moved into #215. It too had a view of the woods. On rare foggy nights, the yellow glow of the lights on the pond turned the fog into a golden haze. Marianne absorbed it with pleasure. She stopped the chemo; the hospital bed came: Wil Luginbuhl, the oncologist, and Hospice helped move us gently into the final weeks, days and hours. On March 7, 2009 Marianne died in seeming peace, children at her side.

The golden fog Marianne delighted in now surrounded me in gloom and I mourned as alone as a lost child. My mind slowly reassembled itself in repeat stages, as a teen, as a dating adult, as a lover and as a husband, now without more than half of myself. My children were in agony. We sat, crept, then hobbled on again, finding life and with it came altered selves. Kendal people (Kendalonians?) were available and I remained overtly appreciative and friendly but separated and inwardly self repairing. My children grieved and patients' needs remained.

In the five years since Marianne's death my life has absorbed Kendal to a greater degree. I've joined, and been asked to join, and do so with increasing appreciation of our special, selected, mildly mixed tribe. We are housed, protected, fed, worried over and expertly managed. I now call it Kendal Island. It has become home, familiar, foibled, fabled, even fantastic. We are all circling the drain and hold imaginary hands as we bob about. Some of us roll, some push, many still walk. We forget, we lose, we wait, and we remember the long ago best. We talk to each other, to our pets and our flowers. Our art smiles to us from the halls and walls. An amazing place.

The Consecrated Cottage
Bob & Betty Warner

I've always loved singing. For me, it is a spiritual experience, blending my bass voice with the sopranos and the altos to create a work of art that floats away in the air when done, leaving both singer and listener feeling connected with each other and the universe. After retirement, I was thrilled to participate in my local church choir, but as time approached for the Kendal phase in my life, I feared that my desire to sing would have no outlet.

As we explored residency at Kendal at Longwood, we came for a two-day "Try Us" experience. (Potential residents are invited to come and stay for three days to experience the community on a trial basis. We highly recommend that every prospective resident do so.) Amazingly enough, Kendal had a chorus! And it was rehearsing the day we visited! Excited and expectant, I joined their rehearsal. Kendal is a community of nearly 400 active and involved adults, so I was surprised to find only 20 or so residents at the rehearsal. These, mostly women ranging in age from ages 70 to over 100, were excited that a male bass singer might someday join them, and they welcomed me warmly. Under the guidance of choir director Sheila, they were doing well for their size and composition, but this choir would not meet my hopes for a challenging opportunity to develop and practice my singing skills. Ah, well, Kendal was still our best choice for a retirement community and perhaps I would find a choir nearby where I could sing.

Sooner than expected, we were offered an ideal cottage, sold our house and were living in a temporary cottage while ours was being renovated. Off I went to my first choir rehearsal and to my surprise and delight, now there were 70 of us in the Kendal Singers, including more basses—male basses. I was again warmly greeted, given my music, and settled into the back row of basses, just behind our neighbor-to-be Ian and between married couple Ellie and Merritt. The concert was to include 14 beautiful songs, varying in complexity, composition age and type. I resolved to learn them quickly, and rehearsed at our temporary home using my computer linked to YouTube for the music. I shared my YouTube links with Sheila and the choir. Many found them helpful.

In between rehearsal and settling in, we watched the progress of our cottage. Kendal had decided that the cottage would be totally redone, and had stripped it to the studs: new plumbing, new electrical, new HVAC. We considered ourselves incredibly lucky to move into a virtually new cottage, but our neighbors-to-be were suffering through the construction noise and traffic, including the deliveries of wall-board and appliances. Though the cottages are remarkably soundproof, the jarring, pounding sounds of hammers and saws permeate most walls. Ian shared with us one day that he had been startled in his bathroom by the chatter of the construction workers, who had torn down most of the wall and insulation between our bathrooms. We were all anxious for the work to be completed. It was to be ready the week before the concert.

The week before the concert also happened to be the date of a dessert party planned by Ian and his wife, Mary Alice. We were invited to join with several other choir members and Sheila (the choir director) for after-dinner cake and song.

As it happened, Betty, my wife couldn't attend the party; she was in New Jersey helping our daughter with our pre-school grandchildren. She missed more than the party.

We were a joyous and noisy group of singers as we walked together from dinner to Ian and Mary Alice's cottage for cake: Ellie and Merritt, Sheila and her husband Hank, Bill and Gail and Ian. Passing our cottage, I offered to use the key I had just received to show the finished cottage. As we tumbled through the door together, we admired and exclaimed at how wonderful it looked, especially the open living room with the vaulted ceiling. Standing under the vaulted ceiling, Merritt commented upon how beautifully our voices were resonating. It turned out that the cottage, devoid of furniture, drapes and rugs, was acoustically live; it felt like being in a large shower or a small cathedral. Six of the group were members of the rounds singers, and all were involved with the Kendal Singers. In that perfect moment of joy and camaraderie, Merritt began singing the beautiful, sacred and well-known round "Dona Nobis Pacem," which roughly translates as "Grant us peace." The rest of us immediately joined in. With great glee, this crowd of celebrating singers touched the walls with their voices and thrilled at the reverberations.

"Grant us peace" echoes still in the walls of our cottage although curtains and furniture have ended the resonance of the song. The spirit of the hymn and of the fellowship will reverberate here throughout our stay. It was indeed a consecration of the cottage by friends with whom we had chosen to spend the remainder of our lives.

Kendal and Quaker Values
Carlie Numi

What are Quaker Values? And how are they manifest at Kendal? These questions arise from time to time on the part of new residents or when visitors are looking at Kendal as a potential place to live. Personally, I think Quaker values do not differ significantly from the values of other religions or belief systems. We list, almost casually, peace, integrity, community, simplicity, equality and stewardship as our basic values. Don't these resonate with the values of other groups—possibly using other words?

Most obviously, we exhibit community in the way resident activities are carried out with no staff to run the programs for those of us living independently. New residents learn about this reality of community living quickly as they are invited to participate in any number of committees designed to enhance the quality of our lives together.

Although we live into all the values to a greater or lesser degree and subject to much personal interpretation, I think we are strongest, and most unique, where community and equality overlap. The respect and caring that residents and staff show for each other are evident in everyday interactions as well as when there is a crisis. Mostly, we remember to be courteous and thoughtful and forgiving, as needed. Staff are unwaveringly patient with residents as we become difficult, forgetful or careless. Residents show interest and concern for staff on a regular basis. There is a familiar banter and friendliness between residents and staff. My sense is that other communities do not foster such close, caring relationships.

One of the most important aspects of Quakerism is not listed as a value. That is the Quaker decision-making process. It begins with a commitment on the part of each person to agree that those assembled are all seeking the best possible resolution to the issue at hand. This means that once one has put forth his / her proposal for a solution, her / his attachment to that proposal takes a back seat while listening with openness and respect to feedback and to other proposals. Giving everyone an opportunity to speak and showing respect are paramount in this process. With good leadership, decisions are usually reached that nearly everyone can feel good about. This process is not easily learned and we do not live up to its ideals as well as we do some of the values listed above.

Quakers make much of their belief that "there is that of God in everyone." Insofar as we can remember that, from moment to moment in our lives, our community will continue to be recognized as a special place.

Is Kendal Good Value?
David Leonard

When my wife, Leslie and I retired, there were many reasons why we and our four children wanted us to enter a respected Continuing Care Retirement Community such as Kendal. Leslie's long widowed grandmother got *younger* with the good fellowship when she entered one in Iowa; my parents were able to remain close to each other when my father developed dementia after they entered another Quaker CCRC here in Pennsylvania; and I always knew they were well-cared for, even though their children were widely dispersed (as are ours) and could visit only infrequently.

However, let me focus here on another question that troubles many families who consider Kendal: isn't it very expensive (if not a luxury) that fritters away the children's inheritance. When Leslie and I were getting ready to retire from the University of California, she went to a set of retirement seminars it sponsored. The specialist on retirement homes advised all of us that it was less expensive to stay at home as long as we could and then go into a nursing home when care was needed. Leslie immediately objected that the inevitable outcome of this recommendation was that you became single, for it was sure to result in the separation of a couple when the health of one of them deteriorated. And at Kendal we have observed that when one spouse *does* inevitably die before the other, he or she receives superb social support from the community of other residents with whom one has built close ties over the years of dinners together.

The flaw in the financial part of the advice was more complicated, however, and deserved careful consideration. Leslie and I were educators and never had much money, so we are very frugal in the way we spend money. We and our children came to have no doubt that Kendal represented a very sound investment. How can this be, you might ask, given the monthly charges and the significant entry fee? Obviously these are more expensive than what it would have cost for us to stay in our home as two healthy seniors. This comparison is illusory, however. The odds that both of us would simply drop dead of a heart attack at home, with no extra hospitalization and nursing home charges, are small and the chances that it would happen to both of us at the same time are infinitesimal. The best of the likely scenarios, had we remained in our home, is that one of us would end up in a costly nursing care facility while the other commuted for visits from home. In other words, we would have died separately, with little social support around us.

The real comparison, then, is not what it would cost us to live in retirement at home now but what it would cost when one of us developed a condition requiring the availability of a nurse. The latter can be very expensive. One of my grandfathers was modestly well-off when he developed Parkinson's. He was cared for at home but that required nurses. In today's dollars the family spent about a million dollars on his care before he died. Very little was left for my grandmother to live on and there was no inheritance for the children.

When Leslie and I chose to invest in a move to Kendal, we reasoned that we were purchasing a dramatic reduction in the risk that one of us would end life impoverished and a burden on our children. Our entry fee really is an annuity on a paid-up long-term care insurance policy. And our monthly charges—which are guaranteed not to rise as we move into more expensive stages of care—are the premiums for all the rest of our long-term care costs. Once we were in Kendal, we were able to cancel the long-term care insurance policies we had started fifteen years earlier. And one of our sons wrote to thank us for sparing him from ever having to have one of those painful talks on how "Mom (or Dad) it really isn't safe for you to remain in your home any longer."

Insurance against risk is never cheap but most of us know that it is wise, and when we are spending it on an organization such as Kendal, which effectively is guaranteeing that we will *never* be unable to afford the care we need, we *and our children* consider that it is a very good value indeed.

Instant Aging
Gabrielle Griswold

The cataract surgery surprise
isn't just clearer vision for eyes.
It's the shock somewhat drearer
of a view in the mirror
that shatters delusion's surmise!

From Past to Present

Carole and I arrived at the Farmhouse together. We opened the door, and the Lohengrin Wedding March began to play (followed by the Hallelujah Chorus). Our neighbors had arranged and hosted a full-fledged reception, complete with music, wine, and congratulations!!

—MARJORIE MCCANN AND CAROLE SMITH

The Four Bears: A Kendal Fable

Hilda Grauman

Many decades ago, four little bears were born in the German part of Alsace Lorraine. The oldest was named Liesel, the second was Martin, the third was Hilde and the wee one was Hans. They were born during a span of five-and-a-half years and grew up close friends even though they fought at times as little bears do. The wee one, Hans, which means John in English, and Jean in French, was their mother's pet. He was loud, funny, and was called by her "Ivan the terrible" after a famous Russian czar. All four bears spoke either in German or in French.

Here we must digress a moment to tell you about their last name, which was "Beer." In the German language "beer" is pronounced "bear," like an animal; the German word for the animal is "br" pronounced the same as "beer." So the four little bears were known in German as the model bear children because they were brought up to be very good. In their parents' library, the Ex-Libris bookplate in the front of each book showed two little bears holding open the pages of the book.

The four Beers and their parents migrated to America. They loved the seven-day trip on a ship even though the seas were stormy most of the time. As they stood on the deck when the ship pulled into New York Harbor in the darkness of an early rainy February morning they waved to the Statue of Liberty with great excitement and anticipation.

In a taxi, with their snouts plastered against the windows to see what they might see, they were astounded that their name, B E E R, was written in neon lights on a number of store windows. When they asked their Papa why that was, he responded that they had arrived in a country which always welcomed new people by writing their names in colorful print on the windows of their shops. They thought that they must have landed in a wonderful country.

The little bears grew up over the decades, each going in a different direction. Initially, they all went to a new French lycée which was situated in a former mansion near Fifth Avenue in New York so that they would not forget one of their mother tongues. The first one to leave the school was the wee bear now called "Jean," as his parents were encouraged to take him away because he was too funny. Martin was the next to leave; he was not charmed by the old French teacher who was a royalist and wanted France to restore a king to the throne. Liesel, now called Lise, was next to go, to become a registered nurse. Hilde, now Hilda, stayed till the end because she lapped up the French classics and had made many friends. She was one of the first graduates of the school and earned a degree called the "baccalauréat."

The decades rolled on, the bears grew up and became interesting people, always full of life, outgoing, energetic, and adventuresome. All married, and had children, so the wider family became large and remained bound lovingly together. And this is where Kendal came into the picture. Wanting to remain together as they were getting older, the Beers knew of a newly founded Quaker retirement community named "Kendal" in beautiful rural Chester County not far from Philadelphia, and they decided that they would aim to live there together for the rest of their lives. Their stepmother was already living there, enjoying many visits from the "Beer tribe" as they now came to be known. As the place had been founded by Quakers, the now-big-bears wondered whether Kendal would accept people with a name like Beer—and there were four of them! They were assured that this would not be a problem and that they would be welcome.

And so the four big bears came, at various intervals, some with their spouses, and with the hope they would live happily at Kendal forever. It seemed to residents that some member of the "tribe" was always running around the campus, and they enjoyed watching the little ones grow up to become big bears like their parents and their stepmother.

One evening as Hilda was walking to her cottage along the Long Walk, she was joined by a brand-new resident whose name was Gabrielle. After just a few steps, as they were becoming acquainted, she realized that when they were little they had been in French lycée in New York together. Gabrielle vividly remembered them, but they did not remember her because she had been an underclassman and "not worth knowing" by the upperclassmen. Gabrielle and Hilda were both delighted discovering this amazing coincidence some sixty years later in Pennsylvania.

A bigger surprise for Gabrielle came the next morning when she saw Hilda again, now in front of the dining room talking with her three siblings. She shouted: "Mais voilà Lise, Martin, Hilda et Jean!!" What a find on her second day here. She was moving into a cottage just three doors from Hilda's, and together they organized a monthly French table to be joined by others whose French was in various stages of fluency or decadence.

At Kendal all four Beers were much involved in the life of the community. They learned new skills, they worked on the trails, they saw more operas on the big screen in the auditorium than they had seen in their previous lives, they learned pottery and a great many other things too numerous to list here.

Lise, who had been a nurse and always cared for others, found many friends whom she could help. As an amateur musician, she made new friends with whom she could play chamber music. Her cottage was open to many folks, the more the merrier.

Martin came to be known as the Mayor of Kendal. He knew everybody, he welcomed strangers in the halls and encouraged them to come to Kendal, he repaired all the broken machines in the homes of kind and gentle ladies.

John became a most productive gardener and organizer of the vegetable gardens and orchards down by the tennis courts. He could not do enough for others, and when his gladioli were in their full glory they cheered up those who were under the weather. He was a loved member of the community.

And so, the little Beers who loved Kendal with all their hearts, lived on happily, not forever, but for many many years, fulfilled with purpose and enjoyment.

Connecting the Circle
Trudy Huntington & Jeanne Whitaker

We first met when we were toddlers, but neither of us remembers that.

TRUDY

In 1934, Jeanne lived with her grandmother in Wooster. Ohio. For Christmas vacation I came to Wooster with my family to visit my grandmother. We were 10 years old. Jeanne's mother and my father had both attended school in Wooster. They knew each other well, as they had lived in the Inky with other missionary children whose parents were "in the field." (The Inky" was shorthand for the humorously named residence, "The Incubator for Monkey Eggs.") Before leaving Wooster, Jeanne and I decided to become pen pals. Unbeknownst to us, my mother had talked to Jeanne's family about my spending the year I was 14 with them in France.

During the following years we exchanged occasional letters and post cards. I was given a book "Little Jeanne of France" which became my favorite. I read and reread the book, trying to imagine what it was like for Jeanne to live in France. Whenever a letter arrived from Jeanne, my mother mentioned that I would visit her when I was 14, but by then France was at war. It seemed obvious to me that instead of my going to France, Jeanne would come to live with us. My mother and father thought that was an excellent idea. Mother said she would write to the Theises as soon as I located Jeanne's most recent address. I finally found it on one of Jeanne's postcards and my mother wrote to her mother, inviting Jeanne to come and live with us.

JEANNE

My family was living in Le Chambon-sur-Lignon, in France, when the war broke out in September 1939. My French father was assistant pastor of the Reformed Church and head of a new secondary school. This was the only co-ed boarding school in France. In addition to the Protestants, many of the students were children of Parisian Jews who wanted a good education and a healthy environment in the mountains for their children. During the war my village not only educated children, but sheltered and helped escape several thousand Jews of all ages.

My mother's American family and friends pressed her to come to safety in the U.S., but she did not want to leave my father. However, my parents entrusted their six eldest daughters to the Unitarian Service Committee, which would accompany a group of children from Marseilles, through Spain and Portugal, across the ocean to New York. Trudy and her mother met us there. All six of us spent Christmas in Swarthmore before each went, as prearranged, to live with a different relative or friend. My good fortune was to spend the war years living with Trudy's family.

We attended Swarthmore High School and college. Later, after graduate school at Bryn Mawr, I taught at Swarthmore College for several years. I discovered Kendal soon after it opened when some of my Swarthmore colleagues and Trudy's Aunt Marylyn retired here.

For many years I taught French at Wheaton College in Norton, Massachusetts. I attended the nearest Friends Meeting, in Providence, Rhode Island, so I moved there when I retired. Trudy would visit me in Providence every spring, after her "cousins' reunion" on Cape Cod. By 2010 she had moved to Kendal and I asked her if she could help me deliver some of the papers I had inherited from my father to the Swarthmore Peace Collection. I spent several days with her here then, discovering all the advantages of continuing care and a wonderful community. My son Mark was equally impressed when he visited and he has made it financially possible for me to join.

I feel very fortunate to be able to live again with my sister by adoption, amid so many interesting people and activities.

TRUDY

I seem to have known about Kendal even before it started. When my beloved Aunt Marylyn Wyse (Robinson) moved here, I visited her every time I came east from Ann Arbor, and each time she urged me to come to Kendal before I was old and she was dead. The more I knew about Kendal the more I thought Jeanne must come too. With my children's urging, I finally moved to Kendal 22 years after my husband and I had signed up.

What I Found at Kendal

I have lived on college campuses most of my adult life, none as beautiful as Kendal's. I love my neighbors' flowers and the bushes surrounding me. I also love the flower arrangements and the paintings and hangings lighting up our common spaces.

The human environment is even more attractive. Friends I have met in our Friends Meeting and in the book groups I joined have been inspiring. I have enjoyed the monthly French table. I am impressed by the talent shared in pre-Kendal memories, poetry and story and play readings. I have also appreciated the discussions held by the Diversity Committee and in the Transition sessions. In a community where we all suffer from diminishments it is reassuring to be encouraged and helped to deal with them.

I am particularly grateful for the fitness center and for Suzanne's balance class.

What I Found at Kendal

As part of my professional life I had lived in various communities, I have lived in the boarding school in which I taught. I have lived in a Hutterite community, and a charismatic Christian community in Canada. I have also lived with the Amish, who are semi-communal.

Though details differ among communities, the successful ones all share common characteristics. However, it was the amalgam of characteristics that attracted me to Kendal. To mention a few: Attempting to put Quaker values into practice. The presence of an active Quaker Meeting. The truly democratic functioning of Kendal, in which the residents make many of the decisions that affect how we spend our time, and what our physical environment looks like. The integration of those with varying physical problems into the life of the community; just because one is confined to a wheel chair does not mean one cannot participate in a committee, make use of the Xerox machine, eat in any dining room or explore the lovely campus on the miles of paved walks. There are always interesting people to talk to, changing flowers, photographs and paintings by residents and local artists. And the well stocked library in which to browse. I like the richness of the community offerings that support both social and individual expression. In other words I am very glad I came to Kendal.

JEANNE AND TRUDY

Not only can we share these advantages with many others, on a personal level a circle is completed. We have matured together and now we are growing old together. We were pen pals from grade school who lived together during World War II. And we are again living together in an extended family.

At Last!
Marjorie McCann & Carole Smith

We have been together since 1990. At the time we made a commitment to each other, April 1990, a commitment was all it was, and all that was possible In April 1992 we had a commitment ceremony, which made the Sunday Inquirer, but that's a story for another time. The City of Philadelphia passed legislation recognizing domestic partnerships in 1996, and we signed up. In 2000, the state of Vermont passed legislation establishing civil unions. We traveled to Vermont

with a few friends and family and had a Civil Union ceremony in Putney, in 2001.

We really thought it was important to be "out." We were
both safe: our families "knew," and so did our employers.
We believed, and still believe, that people in the straight
world who actually know people who are gay are less likely to believe we are bent on undermining society. Plus, we
felt it was important to show younger gay people that a
full and rewarding life was possible.

We watched the progress of the same-sex-marriage cam-
paign, and marveled at the pace of change. But we did not
rush to California, or New York, or Massachusetts. It felt
redundant. And, Congress had passed the Defense of Marriage Act in 1996, which meant that getting married in these
other states would have no impact on us in our home state
of Pennsylvania.

In October 2012, we moved into Kendal.

Then, in 2013, the U.S. Supreme Court, in the *United States
v. Windsor* case, overturned the portion of the DOMA which
said that same-sex marriages, legal in the states where they
were performed, would not be recognized by federal law.
That meant, suddenly, that spouses in same-sex marriages
would be entitled to the same benefits under federal law as
heterosexual spouses. (States still were not required to recognize same-sex marriages solemnized in other states). Within
about 20 minutes, we decided to get married!

We decided to go to Provincetown, Massachusetts (still
could not get married in Pennsylvania), our favorite vacation
spot for many years and with many memories. We arranged
for a Justice of the Peace, invited a few close friends, and
planned a ceremony and party. And, of course, we told our
neighbors here at Kendal.

So off we went to Provincetown.

A couple of days before we left, we got an email from one
of our neighbors, saying that a few folks wanted to "raise a

glass" upon our return, and offering a couple of dates. We picked a date, and replied.

We were married September 30, 2013.

We got another email from our neighbor, saying none of our houses was big enough to fit everyone, so we were having a toast at the Farmhouse.

On that day, Carole and I arrived at the Farmhouse together. We opened the door, and the Lohengrin Wedding March began to play (followed by the Hallelujah Chorus). Our neighbors had arranged and hosted a full-fledged reception, complete with music, wine, and congratulations!! They put on a dinner for 30 people, and there was even a wedding cake. It was so amazing, moving.

When we moved to Kendal, we expected to be accepted as a couple. We never expected to be embraced.

Our Outdoors

I saw a woman with white hair, a large brimmed hat and lace up boots just like mine walking into the woods with a lopper over her shoulders. I knew at that moment this was the place for me. That woman was on her own mission. She had found and freed a stand of native holly trees from the invasive vines that threatened their existence. She's a friend of mine now.

— JOAN STEMMLER

Barbara's Butterflies

Owen D. Owens

My wife, Irene, my brother, John, and I were finishing ice-cream cones outside the Kendal cafeteria when Barbara Hallowell walked by. Barbara is an amazing woman—a naturalist, widely read author, master photographer, and travelogue narrator.

"How are your Monarch caterpillars doing?" I asked.

"Come over to my cottage and see," Barbara responded. Barely able to keep up with her jogging pace, soon we were led into her kitchen.

Over my life I have been in many kitchens. Memories of the fragrance of bread baking and hot dishes bubbling come to mind, but never have I been in a room where people satisfy their hunger and found caterpillars eating their way through milkweed leaves! A little one was chewing away on a big leaf, while bigger, beautifully striped caterpillars rested on twigs placed on the counter.

"This is a once-in-a-lifetime event," I said to myself. "My mother would never have let me bring bugs into her kitchen!"

As though Barbara had read my mind she said, "Monarch butterflies are amazing. They spend the winter in Mexico, then fly north, mate, lay their eggs on plants in the milkweed family, and then die. The next generation hatches, grows, pupates, breaks out of their chrysalises and flies farther north —and then another generation repeats the cycle. In the fall the last generation of monarchs flies south, all the way to

Mexico, where the butterflies cluster together on trees to spend the winter."

"But why do you have these Monarchs in your kitchen?" I questioned.

"Oh, these butterflies are in deep trouble. Their population is collapsing. Twenty years ago there were ninety-seven percent more than there are today!"

"What's happening to kill these amazing butterflies?" I asked.

"Out in the Midwest farmers are planting herbicide resistant genetically modified corn, and spraying fields with herbicides—the milkweed plants are being killed, and the larvae have nothing to eat. Land development throughout the country, moreover, has eliminated vast areas of land Monarchs used for breeding. We should be ashamed of ourselves!"

"Thanks for informing us, but how is it you have brought these caterpillars inside?"

"I love nature," Barbara replied, "and seeing people destroy wonderful creatures like butterflies sometimes makes me almost despair. It seems hopeless, and then I decide to do what I can to help. I plant milkweed plants in my cottage garden—come and look."

We walked out onto the small patio. "Butterfly weeds have these brilliant orange blossoms in mid-summer," she informed us, "and I also have the larger swamp milkweed plants. I find the creamy white eggs the female Monarch laid under a leaf, carefully pull the leaf from the plant, and take the leaves inside where they are protected from predators."

"Look, there's a small caterpillar right there," my brother John observed. The more closely we looked, the more caterpillars we saw. Barbara's little garden was welcoming a lot of Monarch life!

"Come back into my kitchen," she said. "Look, here's a caterpillar that has stopped feeding. Soon it will wander around in a big hurry, like a nomad. Then when it finds a suitable place, the caterpillar spins a thread pad from its mouth, clamps itself to this, hangs upside down like a wrinkly "J". I watch closely and take pictures of each stage of the process. After a day or so the caterpillar wiggles and wiggles until its skin splits where its head was, and a shiny yellow-green chrysalis appears. For several days nothing seems to be happening, but inside the ingredients that made up the caterpillar are reforming into a butterfly.

"That truly is amazing!" I exclaimed.

"I try to keep close track of my caterpillars," Barbara continued, "but two disappeared in their wandering. Look, here's a chrysalis underneath my kitchen counter." We bent down, looked under the counter, and sure enough, there was a shiny green chrysalis! "And there's the other one," as she pointed to the underside of a curtain rod.

"This year two chrysalis changed as I watched," she explained. First they were shiny yellow-green with gold dots around their base. Next the shape and proportions shifted. Then after about six days I could see parts of the butterfly inside."

"How can you be so patient?" we wondered.

"Oh, what's going on is so fascinating I can't wait to see what happens next! I set up my tripod, focus the camera, and get ready for the 'click' that tells me the chrysalis has split. Last year I caught a picture of a Monarch emerging, but this year I was distracted for a moment, heard the 'clicks,' and there they both were!"

"What do you do when the Monarch emerges in your kitchen?" we asked. "Well, first it sits and pumps fluid from its body into its wings, allowing its wings to dry. When I feel it is ready, I extend a finger for the butterfly to climb on, which it usually does, and carry it outdoors, setting it on a flower to dry more. When it feels ready it will fly off."

"One year two took off simultaneously. Twice they circled my head, as though to say 'thanks,' and then flew southwest toward Mexico!"

As we walked home I said to myself, "Next year I'm going to bring nature home to our cottage garden, plant milkweeds like Barbara's, and wait for Monarchs to come and lay their eggs. Also, I'll work with our Kendal/Crosslands staff to make sure our meadows have lots of milkweed species."

We human beings can be greedy, thoughtless destroyers, but we can also use our gifts to help living creatures be fruitful and multiply, emulating our Creator. When a woman brings together scientific knowledge with a naturalist's patient observation, and pictures the generation of life with the eyes of a master photographer, we are indeed blessed. This visit to Barbara Hallowell's kitchen was truly a *once-in-a-life-time event!*

The Thrill of the Trail Team
Joan Stemmler

Naturally, when I came to Kendal, one of the reasons was the approximately 500-acre woods. On our first visit, I saw a woman with white hair, a large brimmed hat and lace up boots just like mine walking into the woods with a lopper over her shoulders. I knew at that moment this was the place for me. That woman was on her own mission. She had found and freed a stand of native holly trees from the invasive vines that threatened their existence. She's a friend of mine now.

Ed and I came to Kendal from the top of the Blue Ridge

Mountains of Virginia. The preservation of the natural beauty of the surrounding six thousand-acre forest bordering the George Washington Forest was a covenanted ideal. Residents of the community, under the leadership of an inspiring field naturalist, became devoted volunteers. We learned the native flora and fauna of Virginia, led hikes, helped maintain the trails, removed invasive plants. I was in the thick of it there.

The first time I went out with Kendal's "trail team" there were a couple of women and more men: we all wore heavy gloves, boots and long pants tucked into our socks to protect against ticks. We carried our clippers, hand saws, loppers, bug spray and water. Less than thrilling is the twice weekly task of cutting back overhanging vegetation, encroaching bushes, and removing fallen branches. Occasionally, high winds, heavy rain, ice storms or hurricanes bring trees down across the trails. Then, the team men go into action, wielding the chain saw, crowbars and saws to open up blocked trails. Mark Swick's maintenance men then can come through with mechanized mowers to smooth the three foot wide path.

In time, I began to meet folks who turned out to be my naturalist teachers about these Pennsylvania woods. They introduced me to the new invasive exotic plants choking much of our native flora. In Virginia, I had met the high altitude invaders, also here in Kendal: Asian stilt-grass, floribunda roses, bull-thistles. Here I first saw the scourge on the coastal plain: autumn olive, mile-a-minute, oriental bittersweet, non-native honeysuckle. We come upon trees or shrubs blanketed with mile-a-minute vines right before our eyes. The native shrub is dying, deprived of light. The killer's seed-carrying berries have not yet ripened. We wrest the attacker's thorny tendrils from the succumbing shrub, pull off its engulfing burden of leaves, gather them together, uproot them if we can. How thrilling it is to restore life-giving air and sun to the now saved shrub.

A team member has completed a new map of all the trails of Kendal and Crosslands which is now printed. Others have installed clearly marked signs indicating all the new and old trails through meadows and woods. The pleasures of this extensive trail system, unique in a CCRC, are many. Frequently folks make their daily constitutionals on the two mile paved path. The "Promenade," suitable in many stretches for wheelchairs and provided with benches, is ideal for restful green views. Bird watchers, exercisers, solitude seekers hike the seven miles of the woods trails. Bi-yearly get-togethers, complete with refreshments, encourage residents to visit the woods and trails, with destinations being one or the other of our two ponds and Bennett Creek.

Our large old canopy trees, oaks, beech, hickories and sugar maples; the understory dogwoods, hollies and spice-bushes; and the wildflowers, ferns, fungi and mosses provide food and shelter for our wild animals, plentiful birds and the population of insects and worms and microbes that keep the whole ecosystem healthy.

For the trail team, getting out in the woods with like-minded people and working in the open air is a joy and a rewarding way to contribute to our community.

Bench Food
Gabrielle Griswold

A bench is a bench is a bench—everywhere except at Kendal. Here, the wooden benches that line our walkways morph, in summertime, into objects touched with magic. Elves, it would seem, come in the night (or at least when no one is looking), and deposit troves of fresh produce from Kendal gardens on their slatted wooden seats. One day it might be lettuce which mysteriously appears on a bench somewhere, another day ripe tomatoes, another day string-beans, fresh mint, or edible chrysanthemums. Toward the end of the growing season, it could be zucchini, peppers, even Chinese pears. You can never predict what will turn up next. As everyone knows, farm-fresh and local make for the best eating, and these *very* local fruits and vegetables are the freshest anywhere. No farm-stand product is same-day fresher than they are. Tasty, too.

In fairy tales, elves are unknown to mortals except for the evidence of their good deeds. But *our* "elves" have names and faces we would recognize—those of our own hobbyist gardeners, who, in Kendal plots, grow not only vegetables and fruits but also herbs and flowers. Some portion of their crops they take home for their own use, but Bench Food is what they generously share with the rest of us who do *not* garden.

"Hooked" at Kendal
Bob Parker

It was the first full summer Carolyn and I had spent at Kendal, having arrived the previous fall. Our California daughter and her two children were visiting us. Michael was 13 and his sister, Itzel, was 10. Michael had brought his newly acquired fishing rod and reel with him and was anxious to try it out. We immediately thought of Dudley Campbell, who was an avid fisherman and the perfect mentor to guide Michael in using his new equipment. Dudley had a number of places in the area where he went to fish, but his favorite on the Kendal campus was Spear Pond. One could see him frequently on the pond's shores casting for the several varieties of fish, including large-mouth bass. It was strictly a catch and release pond which suited him fine.

Dudley took Michael down to Spear Pond on their first outing and soon found out that Michael had a very adequate rod and reel for a beginner, but did not have any lures that would allow him to cast out into the pond. He looked in his tackle box and found just what Michael needed, a sleek black and yellow lure with wicked three pronged hooks at either end. He then spent time teaching Michael how to cast the lure accurately so that it would land in spots where there might be fish. Soon Michael was casting fairly accurately and actually caught several small fish. Dudley told Michael that he could use the lure while he was visiting at Kendal, but he would like it back when Michael returned home. After they had been fishing together a few times, Michael asked us if he could go alone. We had encouraged him to always have someone with him when he went.

On a day Dudley wasn't available, I agreed to go with Michael. I said that he could fish while I was doing some work nearby in the lower garden and that I would check on him from time to time, but that we would head home at noon for lunch. Noon came and I found Michael at the southwest corner of the pond. He had had some luck earlier and had caught and returned several small fish.

I told Michael it was time to have lunch and we needed to get back to the cottage. He said he wanted to make one last cast into an area of the pond that looked interesting. I agreed, and as soon as the lure hit the surface of the pond there was a surge of water as a good sized fish hit the surface and splashed back into the pond. The line went taut and Michael started reeling in what appeared to be a fairly large fish. He soon had it near the shore and as he lifted it out of the water we saw that it was a large mouth bass about 12 to 14 inches in length. The fish was jumping around trying to get loose as Michael held his line towards me to help him unhook the fish and return it to the pond.

Unfortunately the fish was caught by both triple hooks at the ends of the lure, one on either side of its big mouth. We didn't have any pliers to grab the hooks by, so I asked Michael to hold the fish while I tried to get the hooks out. By this time the fish was getting desperate and Michael was having trouble holding it while I was gingerly trying to unhook it. I had almost succeeded when the fish gave a very strong jerk and out came the hooks.

However, as Michael threw it back into the pond, we both saw what had ensued when it had jerked loose. I was firmly hooked in both hands, my left thumb being impaled by the hook at one end of the lure and my right palm had the hook from the other end well embedded in the skin in the middle! Michael still had the fishing rod line attached to the lure and we didn't have anything to cut it.

By this time we were quite a sight, Michael holding the rod with the line attached to the lure and the lure between my hands making me look like a supplicant. All I could think was to get back to the cottage as quickly as possible where I had needle nosed pliers that might be used to pull out the hooks. We took off from the pond, around the Wellness Center and the end of the Health Care wing, coming into the back side of our cottage, arriving at the patio door. We must have been a strange sight, Michael in the lead, followed by me with my outstretched hands, now bleeding a little, attached to the line from Michael.

We shouted for someone to open the door. My grand-daughter, Itzel, came running and when she saw us, all she could say was "gross," and shouted for her grandmother to come quick. As soon as Carolyn appeared I told her to get the needle-nosed pliers and something to cut the line. Once I was detached from Michael's line, Carolyn was able to extract the hook in my right hand, but couldn't budge the hook in my left thumb. She then called Resident Care and asked if anyone there could remove a fishing hook. They told her if I came up right away, Dr. Soraruf would still be there and had experience removing fish hooks.

We rushed up to the Center, still in my dirty garden clothes with the lure cradled in my left hand. The nurses cleaned up my hand and Dr. Soraruf injected a local anesthetic and quickly had the fish hook out of my thumb. I was very fortunate that he had still been there; otherwise we would have had to go all the way to the emergency room in West Chester.

After cleaning up the lure we handed it back to Dudley with thanks for a very exciting time using it. It had been quite effective in hooking fish and certainly my hand.

That Christmas I got Michael a lure much like the one Dudley had loaned him. Several years later after Dudley died, I met his wife Ros in the Center. She handed me a little package and said it was for Michael. It contained a few lures that Dudley had used and she wanted to give them to someone who would appreciate them. Thanks to Ros, Dudley's love of fishing was still being shared with others.

Kendal's Animal Kingdom
Gabrielle Griswold

When Noah stocked his Ark, his priority was preservation. Nowadays we also know that the presence of animals can actually be therapeutic for humans. At Kendal, animals abound. Some of us keep them as pets, ranging all the way from the usual warm-and-fuzzies like dogs and cats to—at one time!—non-fuzzies like gastropods. We even have a live-in therapy cat who pays regular visits to full-nursing-care patients, to sit on the laps of those who relish a furry cuddle. Like Noah, we have pet birds—and maybe somewhere pet fish—which flutter or swim in their respective cages and tanks, to cheer the eyes and hearts of passersby in some of Kendal's hallways.

No lions or tigers here, but as a Certified Wildlife Habitat site, we also host a variety of native animals on our wooded grounds. Most of them we seldom see, but they are there: deer, foxes, rabbits, and probably a host of unsuspected others, moving mysteriously beyond the trees. At twilight, what more peaceful sight than a herd of deer silently emerging from the woods to graze on the borderland between lawn and forest?

As, also, an accredited arboretum, our gorgeous trees are home to numerous wild birds: colorful cardinals, bluebirds, goldfinches, hummingbirds, and so many others that we compile lists to keep track of our sightings, sometimes for our own information, sometimes as participants in Audubon Society bird counts.

Noah would certainly have included butterflies in his Ark, so we must include them too, and—in early summer—fleets of fireflies that drift through the air like fallen stars. So, maybe it's not an ark we live in here, but guess what? Whatever form they take, our animals add grace, beauty, and sometimes healing, to our lives.

An Adventure in the Woods
Terry Engeman

Kendal is perhaps unique among the high concentration of retirement communities in this part of the country in that we enjoy a spacious, tree-filled campus bordered by several acres of woodland through which walking trails are maintained by and for residents. When I first arrived, over a decade ago, I found a map on which was marked a perimeter path for safe strolling away from the service roads. I looked for this path but could not find it. When I inquired where it might be, I was told the map was only a suggestion; there was no actual pathway. (The Dwyer Promenade was constructed a couple of years later.)

Nevertheless, I set off one day to explore the woods, entering near Parking Lot 11 on the Woods Trail. As the sounds of civilization faded, all was peace. Birds twittered. Leaves rustled. Twigs cracked underfoot. The trail was marked by fallen logs laid alongside it and sometimes there was a choice to be made: here the Ridge Trail branched off to the right, there the Fallen Tree Trail dipped down into a sort of ravine.

Wanting to see as much as possible, I left the marked trail and picked my way through the leaves, skirting dead branches and climbing over logs, eager to immerse myself fully in this unspoiled "wilderness."

At the bottom of the fairly steep slope I could see a pond in the distance. I made my way over to it, with some difficulty as there were thorny bushes here and there and I was, unwisely, wearing only shorts and sandals. The pond appeared to be isolated, as there were no signs of habitation. After viewing it I started back the way I had come…and realized that I was completely lost. I had no idea where the trails were, or which direction to go to find one.

Crossing a small stream, Bennett's Run, I slipped on a rock and scratched my legs and hands on the clustered brambles. I realized that if I should, say, sprain my ankle, there was no way anyone would find me in this remote corner of the campus, or even know that I was missing. (My daughter scolded me, and insisted that I get myself a cell phone for just such a possible emergency.)

As I wandered I recalled an incident when I was nine years old and hiking with others through the woods a few miles from our farm on an isolated Vermont mountaintop. I stepped off the trail to answer a call of nature, while the others moved on and soon were out of sight. Having taken care of business I went to rejoin the group, only to realize I could not find the faint path we'd been following. Apparently not having noticed that I was absent, no one was looking for me or calling.

Although of course worried, I was a sensible child and recalled that one should always walk downhill to find signs of civilization. Faintly in the distance came the sounds of a small sawmill, where I knew there would be people I could ask for help. Stumbling resolutely through the woods, I soon arrived at a dirt road and trudged along it, to find my group anxiously waiting. "You should have told us you were stopping!" they scolded.

Now I was lost again, with no sounds to guide me: no passing cars, no human voices, just birdsong and rustling leaves. Freeing myself from the clinging brambles I clambered back up the slope, recalling apprehensively that there was a waste water (read: sewage) treatment spray field somewhere in the woods. I had seen the spray heads and began to fear that the system would suddenly turn on and drench me with…well, it didn't bear thinking about. Would there be some kind of warning signal, such as supermarkets use when they are about to spritz the fresh produce? Hardly likely. I resolved to give the spray field a wide berth!

After 10 or 15 minutes of wandering I did finally come upon a trail, and with relief followed it over to the Crosslands service road, and from there back to familiar territory.

Since then I have, armed with my cell phone (though whether it would work down in the ravine is questionable), explored other trails, always finding something new to appreciate: a spring flower, a woodpecker, a deer's hoof print, the rain-filled streamlet. Recently I discovered the Sunrise Trail, which loops through an area where until quite recently there used to be houses. Here are shady woods, a pond, bountiful raspberry bushes in season, a sunny hillside with a bench for resting, an abandoned vegetable garden, and a number of mysterious green tubes containing tree saplings, planted in odd locations. The Old Kennett Meeting House burial ground is visible through the trees, a historic site where a number of Kendal residents have chosen to spend eternity. Nearby, a long, perfectly straight row of huge pine trees, planted for who-knows-what original purpose, marches across the landscape. One comes back out into the sunshine near the new cottages feeling refreshed and reconnected with nature.

How fortunate we are to be able to "get away" in our own back yard! It is hard to get lost, as the trails are clearly marked. But it could happen, so carrying a cell phone or whistle is only sensible. Best idea: carry the pocket-size trails map, available at the reception desk.

Ducking Mother's Day
Janet Spencer

Mother's Day again, and, as usual, we had no children visiting or planning to visit. I had always said that Mother's Day was an invention of florists to build business, and that was enough said to dismiss it. But it was Mother's Day, and my celebration that morning consisted of taking our border collie/cattle dog mix, Kerri, for an extra mid-morning walk in the woods. There was a bit of an empty feeling because I had so effectively run down Mother's Day to my own three absent children.

Off we strode, down the promenade toward Spear Pond, where we sometimes bore witness to the flapping ascent of a great blue heron or the fast exit of a little green heron in fear of discovery. We usually headed into the woods for a nice descent into leafy paths under tall tulip poplars, oaks and maples, across a little stream where Kerri liked to get her feet wet and lap a little of nature's real water. I looked forward to entry into this other world, another part of Kendal. Walks in the woods always provided refreshment and a special sort of grounding.

As we started around the pond, approaching the woods, I heard a commotion just up the bank of Spear Pond. Looking back, I saw something dark and moving on the ground inside a three-sided net enclosure protecting a new planting from the ever-voracious deer population. What to do? I had Kerri with me. She was always keen to investigate wildlife rather too vigorously. Backtracking toward the ruckus, I told Kerri to "Stay back!" and approached the netting. Just when I was several yards away a small adult duck burst out from under the netting and quacked her way down to the water below. "OK," I thought. "That will take care of the problem." Kerri only observed. Good dog.

We continued our walk in the woods. But half-way around the pond, again, there was further commotion within the netting. Back we went, more warnings to Kerri to stay away, and sure enough there was something else inside the netting. Close-up, it appeared that a whole pile of duck-lings was trapped inside! Quickly, I raised the netting and the crowd of peeping ducklings inside was on its way—bumbling, tumbling, stumbling—down across the foot path, through the weeds next to the water, and down to Mom, who was calling them…a distressed nasal whoo, whoo, whoo…from below. Some ducklings got stuck in the corners of the netting, so I had to gently scoop them free. There were too many ducklings to count in this scene of total confusion. They appeared to be wood ducks. We had seen a mated pair lounging in the upper pond, up the hill from Spear Pond. The nest must have been on the edge of Spear Pond, and Mama and newly hatched babies were on their way to the upper pond when they encountered the net barrier which they apparently chose to go under instead of around.

The whole brood made it safely into Spear Pond in response to their Mom's constant calling. Now all bunched up, they appeared to be one organism swimming around in the water, getting their bearings. Wood ducks are small, and the babies very small. Mama and babies were so bunched up that it was still hopeless to count them, but there must have been about a dozen ducklings.

Kerri and I went on our way into the woods, figuring that they would survive better with as little human and canine company as possible. Kerri had been her usual good dog, and, responding to my admonitions, hadn't tried to go after them. I was very pleased with our rescue operation. In fact, the episode made my Mother's Day. I felt I was the godmother to a bevy of baby wood ducks.

The next day, sure enough, we spotted the wood duck family in the upper pond. Compared with two families of Canada geese with whom they mingled, the wood ducks were really small. As days went by the goose babies grew fast, but the wood duck babies remained very small, perfect embodiments of vulnerability. They still formed a tight bunch around Mom.

A week after their rescue from the netting, again on a dog walk, my husband, Doug, and I spotted the wood ducks. Mom and very small babies were swimming inside the reed bed, a part of our water treatment system here at Kendal. The reed bed had recently undergone its periodic cleaning and re-stocking with a new sand base, newly planted reeds, and a fresh fill of water. There were at least three vertical feet of cement wall above the water line that the birds would have to scale in order to get out of the reed bed. But those little ones could not fly yet! They were stuck! Mama was swimming in circles and calling anxiously. Again, what to do?

Well, we found a couple of six-inch wide, eight foot long planks, and Doug shoved one end of each into the muck under the water and rested the other end on top of the cement wall. Perhaps the ducks could figure out how to climb the planks to escape to the larger world once more. Since we had sort of stolen the planks from their job of holding plastic down over a pile of plywood down the hill, and since we had breached the reed bed's surrounding fence, we called Mark Swick, our Grounds Supervisor, to confess our sins. I related to him the original Mothers' Day rescue story. Mark is a duck lover himself. His reaction was wonderfully supportive. He voiced no objection to our break-in, and no problem with the planks, he said, and he would check on the situation himself that afternoon. Later in the day we also checked, and were overjoyed to see the ducks were no longer stuck inside the reed bed. In fact, they were back in the upper pond. And we noticed that the netting that had trapped them on Mother's Day had been removed, no doubt courtesy of Mark.

A couple of weeks later I saw Mama duck again in the reed bed, no babies in tow. She appeared to be taking a break from baby-tending, and had left her children in the upper pond with the geese! I swear, she had signed out to the geese, trusting them to protect her charges against the hazards lurking all around. Anyway, they all existed congenially together, always intermixed, large and small together. The geese could have lectured Mama duck about child care. Whereas the geese constantly and proudly accompanied their babies, Dad in front and Mom in the rear of the line, the Mama duck was very casual about watching over her brood. By this time the ducks were no longer in a bunch, and could be seen scattered about a rather large area among the lines of geese. Daddy duck was nowhere to be found.

Even later, after the babies could fly, I saw Mama and offspring in the reed bed. This time they all flew out to the upper pond, no problem at all. They were ready to take off to faraway places, and we would not be seeing them much again. Eight of the approximately dozen chicks had survived so far, a very good number considering the hazards abounding: hawks, snapping turtles, raging electrical storms, hungry foxes, cats, dogs, weasels, a reed bed entrapping ducklings, and pesky netting set out by well-meaning humans, among them.

By now it is September. Both geese and ducks have gone, leaving behind an empty pond and the satisfaction of knowing we helped keep up the wood duck population a little bit with our rescue efforts. They provided us a great celebration of Mother's Day, found by chance on the way to a walk in the woods.

Steve Angell's Summer

Allan Brick

Steve says, I am going to work
with the Conference children,
nine and ten year olds.

Play games, talk—
they have ideas. I
can't bear what's happening

to children in Iraq,
Palestine, Sudan,
living in terror.

I reply, Before adolescence.
He says, Yes, now
is the time: they can think.

Into his eighties, head
bent over, neck locked, stooped,
he sits on a walkway bench.

Just a little rest, he explains:
my angina kicks in.
Steve's normal work these days

is at the prisons—sessions
with prisoners, guards, learning
alternatives to violence.

Pausing on my walk, I
look down at him,
so hunched he can't look up.

Mornings at this year's Conference
the Quaker nines and tens
will come to know Steve.

Favorite Places

"Yes," I said. "I'm interested in learning to weave." Something profound had begun in that moment. A whole new love affair between me and this life-giving activity had begun! —GABRIELLE KIMMEL

The Gateway Shop

Annie Hazard

The Gateway Shop was my entry into volunteering at Kendal. The sign on the door read: "Salespeople Needed: Ask at the Desk." I figured that since I had been a salesgirl at B. Altman & Co. during my high school and college summers, I could do that and get to meet lots of new people. So, I asked at the desk and was immediately signed up!

"May I help you?" I asked a slightly built woman who had entered with her walker.

"Oh, yes, please," she said. "I've forgotten my glasses, and I can't read the labels. I need some new batteries."

"Oh, I can help you," I answered. "Come over to this shelf." We walked over to the battery and sundries shelf.

"What size do you need?" I asked.

"Hmm," she was trying to remember. "I think C's or D's, but I'm not sure." She looked puzzled.

"What are they for?" I asked.

"My flashlight, so I can see at night to get to my bathroom."

That would be a D," I answered. "But, maybe you'd like to try this little one—all it takes is light to charge it, either electric or sunlight works." I showed her the new little flashlights that had come in recently.

"Oh," she brightened up. "And it's not so heavy." She was trying it out and looked pleased. "I'll get this one. I'm going to tell my friends about this flashlight," she said as she left.

The jewelry is a wonderful buy: watches for $10.00-15.00 are decorative, coming in colors and various styles. Also popular are necklaces and earrings.

"Oh, you've gotten more nice jewelry," announced a customer one day.

"Yes," I answered. "She brought them in this morning."

"May I try this set on?"

"Of course," I answered. We had a mirror available so she could view herself in it. The gold and silver beads were elegant and had tiny dangling earrings to go with them.

"Oh, I love it, but I want to try this one on, too." The customer went on to the next set and modeled that one. Then she went back to the first set, unable to make up her mind.

"Perhaps you'd like to buy both sets," I suggested.

"How much would that be?" wondered my customer.

"Well, let's see: $78.00 plus tax and the other is $84.00 plus tax." I knew she could easily afford it.

She looked a little surprised but said "Well, it's not over $200 and I'm going to give one set as a Christmas present. I'll take both!" Wow! That was a big sale!

Less expensive items like candy, gum, Tums, and cough drops have regular customers. Some come in every day for their "chocolate fix" or "gum purchase." Since I am also the buyer for Candy and Sundries I pay attention to which of these need to be replaced. We've had runs on Dove dark chocolate bars, M & M's, large York peppermint patties, and Peanut Chews.

"How come you don't have any sugar free candy?" a customer asked one day.

"Well, I'll see what I can do," I answered looking it up in my suppliers catalogue.

"Here they have lemon flavored or mixed fruit flavored sugarless drops. Which would you like?"

"Lemon," she stated and so we ordered some.

Of course, our mainstay is cards. Many of us are parents and grandparents, and most of us have lifelong friends, who at this stage need timely attention. Birthdays, anniversaries, holidays, and especially "get well!" are the market.

"I love these cards with the animals making silly faces," a customer said one day. "Do you have any more?" I checked the drawers for the extra cards and just found copies of the ones on the display rack.

"Sorry, looks like this is all of the ones with the animals," I said. The customer seemed annoyed, but took out a bunch of the ones she was looking at. She placed them on the counter, and kept checking the backs.

"Are you looking for something special?" I asked.

"Just the prices," she answered, shaking her head. "Well, these don't seem to be right" and walked out of the shop! All the cards were left on the counter. I was gathering them up to put them back, when suddenly she reappeared.

"Oh, don't put them away," she said. "I'm going to buy a couple of them!"

Sometimes it's the cash register that gives us a workout. If one hits the 00 key instead of the 0 key twice, nothing works and the cancel button is used. But with practice and good humor it all comes together in the end. In fact, practice and good humor are key to working in the Gateway Shop.

The Weaving Room
Gabrielle Kimmel

We had just moved in and I was off to find that room. As I turned the corner, I could see that the door was open. I was very excited, but I wasn't sure what to expect. Could I ever learn this complicated new craft? I was familiar with macramé, crewel, crocheting, knitting, embroidery and all types of sewing. I'd even once sewn a plaid winter coat. I was a patient, careful doer of many crafts. But this one that I'd never tried fascinated me. The amazing colors and patterns were fueling my imagination and the prospect was really speaking to me. The complete mystery for me was how the finished products come to reality. (After two years, I'm still not sure exactly *how* it happens.) As I looked into the room, I wondered how I could possibly learn and master this new craft—dish towels and table runners and rugs and tapestries (pictures magically appearing in the midst of the threads).

When Ernie and I passed through this room as we toured Kendal, I said to myself, "I'm going to do that! I'm going to learn to weave!" Now that we had moved in, I was anxious to set eyes again on this lovely large room. There they were, lined up like soldiers of various heights, quietly waiting for action: the looms, owned by Kendal, or current weavers, or donated, or loaned by former weavers.

Light flooded in the windows and it was silent as I stepped into the room. I peered at samplers on the wall and books on shelves. Everything was as I remembered, only more fascinating. I was hooked.

"Hello, can I help you?" Suddenly a voice from somewhere deep in the room. A small woman stepped out from behind a lovely blond, medium sized loom. I had no idea anyone was there. She had been completely absorbed and hidden, not talking, which is the custom in the weaving room.

"Yes," I said, "I'm interested in learning to weave." Something profound had begun in that moment. A whole new love affair between me and this life-giving activity had begun. And equally, this very moment was the beginning of a relationship of affection and appreciation for this woman who stepped out from behind her loom.

Alice Haw is my mentor and inspiration. She embodies the best teaching skills; she knows when to give advice and how to back away and let me do it myself. Sometimes it feels like being thrown into the pool—sink or swim—but it really works. That's how I've learned. She herself learned to weave eight years ago when she came to Kendal. In the same way she was taught by Charlotte Boucheron and others. Her teachers and mentors are now mostly retired from the room, but they stop by once in a while. Charlotte and Jan M. and Marian, and Mary and Joan. And then there are all the ghosts whose names are on the looms or on the shuttles or on the samplers or books, wonderful helpful spirits. How can the few of us now weaving fill the space of these forces from the past?

Nowadays we have several weavers in the room, all quietly throwing shuttles or loading bobbins or setting up to start a new project. Getting started, called "warping the loom" is the most complicated, difficult and crucial part of weaving. The "warp" thread goes lengthwise on the fabric and the "weft" goes across. You throw the shuttle to create the weft. My first project was a wool scarf in soft blues and grays with a fleck of turquoise, a gift I finished in time for Christmas for my husband Ernie. Through several more projects, I've learned a whole new vocabulary: warp and weft, tabby and twill, huck lace and many more fascinating and enlightening words. It's like arriving in a new country—you learn the language to survive.

Some of the present occupants of the room are: Luis, a talented member of the Kendal staff, who made a beautiful huck lace shawl to send to his mother in Mexico. He is now embarking on learning to make a tapestry. Alice Long, a veteran weaver, is described by Alice H. as our "most meticulous weaver, the one to be emulated." She is renowned for making material for beautiful jackets and is still turning out wonderful "monks belt" dish towels. She occupies a cheerful spot by the window.

So here is the question: Will I ever turn out a unique and beautiful tapestry? I hope so. I hope to be weaving for many years. But, pondering the word "tapestry," I am struck by the comparison with the people at Kendal. What a beautiful, diverse, funny, hope-filled, generous minded and interesting group of people are surrounding me in this adventure of living at Kendal. Even if I never produce that piece of fabric, the tapestry is here all around me.

10,000 Books
Allan Brick

Kendal at Longwood, the first of the Kendal continuing care communities, has celebrated its 40th year. It is notable for its arboretum and walking trails, its proximity to Longwood Gardens, its location in the land of Andrew Wyeth, its health services, its caring staff, and its traditions of residents caring for each other. Some of the residents and staff are Quaker. All are affected by the Quaker values of the equality of all people and working in behalf of people throughout the world.

I was aware of much of this in general terms before I moved in. But what blew off the top of my getting-older head when I first visited was the library! Now, more than a decade later, the library continues to amaze me. A half dozen or so of residents who were formerly professional librarians at work cataloguing, shelving, and culling the books (limited space means we have to continually get rid of books of lesser importance to make space for new ones). The Book Selection Committee orders about 25 new books each month. While the collection stays close to the overall number of 10,000, we are particularly strong in history and biography, continuously leavened by the works of new scholars and popularizers. The categories of literature, politics, current affairs, science, and religion are kept going; American history, the Civil War, and the American Revolution are particularly well represented.

There is a disproportionately large collection of romantic fiction, which genre also plays a substantial role in the "large print" and the audio sections. I hasten to add that we don't spend money ordering romance; moreover, we draw the line when it comes to shelving donated bodice-rippers of doubtful literary merit. Though we don't buy them (they are contributed), we probably have every book that the endlessly prolific Danielle Steele ever wrote.

In this regard, I think of Mildred Corey, one of Kendal's founding residents. Mildred was maybe most famous for her insistence, every night in the dining room, that the young people waiting on table find her coffee ice cream. If, having appealed to the dining room director, they reported, "There isn't any coffee ice cream available tonight, Miss Corey," she would respond, "Steve has some in the freezer downstairs. Go and get it." But she was also famous for her long addiction to Danielle Steele. You could find her name, often more than once (how could anyone, even this fan, differentiate from one to another of these novels?) on the card in a Steele book. Mildred once sitting with me at the dinner table filled in the lull while the beleaguered young waiter went in search of coffee ice cream by producing a long typewritten letter that Danielle Steele herself had once written to Mildred in response to a letter of appreciation, no doubt one of the many thousands of fan mail letters that Steele received annually. This responding letter was a personal letter of two full pages; I found it wonderfully thoughtful reading. I was in awe of this realm of performers and their fans, a large world of which I know nothing.

Soon after moving in I was invited to join the Book Selections Committee. It is by far the most independent power-broker position I could ever dream if holding. (After all, if I were President, the Pentagon and the Kochs would tell me what I could do—no real power in that). We bring in book reviews to recommend new books, and we advocate for writers we already respect and, yes, want more of. One of our members is very strong on works of nonfiction and fiction that feature dogs, cats, fish, elephants (a sudden elephant niche these days), and perhaps even butterflies. She passionately makes her case: this kind of book "flies off the shelves."

There is a similar justification for our couple of specialists on books about horticulture and, more widely, the natural environment. For several us who are more up front political, environmentalist radicalism is always a good basis for a new selection. I myself specialize in recommending works of fiction and memoir. The Committee doesn't always support my candidates, but when I really want to read something that I know is of great merit I do heavy research and attempt to carry the day. Thus we are strong on the full literary list of current fiction. The only barrier in ordering a new important novel, and indeed for ordering anything, is that it not be too very many pages long—weight won't fly off of the shelves, won't even amble.

One of my own addictions puts me on a very democratic footing with a large number of our library users—that is our very substantial collection of mysteries. It occupies two wings of one of the corners of the large library room. Mysteries are hardbacks and paperbacks, many of them donations (screened by the Selections Committee), by the very wide spectrum of those who write for this huge market. We spend up to a quarter of our new books budget on these, bowing to the tastes of the escapist readers in our community.

I am one such. I justify such adventurous stuff ("junk" one of my most intimate friends calls it) for after dinner getting sleepy time. Thus we have the full collection of Robert Parker's Spenser novels. And, more respectably, we have many books by the best British mystery writers, led of course by P.D. James and Ruth Rendell, gloriously followed by Peter Lovesy, Peter Robinson, and Ian Rankin, as well as such wonderful new arrivals as Kate Atkinson, Benjamin Black and Tana French. Along with one's latter day passion for history and biography, such escapism, personally greedily defined, makes life very much worth living.

In addition to the wheelchair ghost of Mildred over there browsing the romances, for me the most significant patron is the still-quite-alive woman who spends lots of time after her dinner standing in front of the New Books section. She riffs through the pages of some. She tells anyone in earshot, "There is nothing here I want to read." You suggest something that would suit her, well, tastes, say by Maeve Binchy, or Ann Tyler, or even, stretching it a bit, Toni Morrison, and she says, "Oh, I read that." Or more credibly she says, "Oh, I tried that one." There is something very fine about this woman standing her eternal vigil staring at the New Books shelf, and I find it luminously sacred. Hope must spring. Some day (which I admit won't come) she may upgrade; she may choose and actually read and tell her friends about it with great enthusiasm, one by Doctorow, or McEwan, or even Marilynne Robinson (who, arguably, shares her values of virtue and religion). She will not, I feel sure, gravitate to the Romances section.

The library merits its big annual budget allotment from the Kendal Residents Association. Recently, in the KRA meeting responsible for the next year's budget, there was a serious attempt to cut the library budget. This move was understandable since the appropriate Committee chair had not submitted the full accounting requested for the next year's expenditures. The library angels, taking high ground, had simply submitted their summary to the effect that 'same as last year' would do it. When push came to shove, the budget committee got everyone's attention by formally recommending a substantial reduction in the budget. It was a moment that reminded me—same fervor and (if you interpret) same humanist cause—that millions of people all over the nation had expressed when—to no avail—we had gone out on the streets to protest George Bush's imminent invasion of Iraq. This one was, of course, winnable. Voices were raised. Literate voices. People rose in full credit to the tradition and rhetoric of our founding fathers—our American heroes who themselves held a well stocked niche in the Kendal Library.

Grampa, I Won't Mind Getting Old

Bill Van Wie

Four years ago, as we were going through our house in New York to prepare for our move to Kendal, I brought out cork bulletin boards to give to two of our grandchildren who were staying with us. Our 8-year-old granddaughter said, "Grampa, it's not Christmas or our birthdays; why are you giving these to us now?"

I told her, "Remember, we're getting ready to move."

She said "Oh yeah, you're going to that hotel where they take care of old people!"

Then we moved to Kendal. Last April, all four of our grandchildren were staying with us in our cottage. We had planned to take them on visits to local attractions including Longwood Gardens and the Delaware Natural History Museum. But we never left the campus! They walked around the grounds. They ate in the coffee shop and the dining room. They met many of our friends. They found the Center, with the indoor pool, and the library, and the table tennis, and the indoor bocce game, and the chess game, puzzles and other indoor games. They were too busy and happy here to leave the campus.

On the last day of their visit, as we walked back to our cottage, our 14-year-old grandson said "Grampa, I won't mind getting old."

Make Your Move!

Ruth McMurry

Kendal Reporter, December 8, 2008

MAKE YOUR MOVE

When rumors began to circulate that I had decided to move to Cumberland, our assisted-living unit, the feedback to me was distinctly various. It ranged from a forthright, "Are you crazy?" to the diplomatic, "You will be a role model for us all...I guess," to the enthusiastic, "You'll love it!" Some just said, "Why?"

Sixteen years had passed since I had moved into #11, and in that interval I had moved from enthusiasm about weeding and caring for my 3-ft. perimeter to arthritic knees and detestation of the grass that had moved into the ground cover that was my ultimate solution to the Garden Beautiful. My earlier hope that I was destined to become a published writer was dampened by rejection letters and trips to Barnes & Noble. All those books? Who needs more? Forget it. I resigned from Women's Ink and put a dust cover on my typewriter. Furthermore, I was getting old. Walks to the Center, to the nearest laundry, to the nearest trash disposal, all inconsequential earlier, were now a drag.

I knew that my arthritic knees would profit from water exercise, but by the time I walked to the pool, undressed, exercised, dressed again, walked home and collapsed on the couch, the morning was gone. Exercise to live? OK. Live to exercise needs some more thought. Even—don't laugh—my hair style had come to the end of a long, unsuccessful run. I was eager to turn my life around. Yo! Cumberland!

Now I have a smallish but delightful room looking out on some of the loveliest trees on the planet. I am directly across from a trash room and 15 steps from a laundry with a machine that dispenses its own detergent. I am 200 steps from the therapy pool and my exercise class. I can have breakfast in a dining room looking out on a superbly designed and maintained garden. The cook does some of the most delicately perfect poached eggs and crisp bacon in town. I sit like Queens of the May, waiting for my order and feeling like a character in a novel or film. My room is cleaned once a week, not twice a month. Calcium pills and Vitamin E capsules are put gratis into my hand. There is no phone bill. I no longer have to struggle into walking shoes and a jacket to go home when the weather is unforgiving.

But what about closet space for a wardrobe admittedly out of control? There is a storage space for each Cumberland resident in the "Cage" on the first floor. Put your out-of-season clothing down there. There is a small but useful six-shelf cabinet in the bathroom and two accessible shelves in the closet. It has slowly become apparent to me that one doesn't need all the things that were once defined as essential.

So much for the Rosy Scenario of an early move to Cumberland. How about the Cautionary Tale of a move too-long delayed? When discarding many of one's prized possessions becomes inevitable, and the ability to make decisions is almost too great an effort. Still worse, when no one seems to want one's prized possessions and they must go to the Goodwill.

If one waits too long, the decisions must be made by family and Kendal staff. Things are shoe-horned in somewhere, but where? Where is the Christmas card list? Where is the Certificate of Title to the car, which can't be given away until it is found? Where are your insurance documents, your will, the Durable Power of Attorney? The feelings of helplessness in such a situation are a powerful argument for moving early rather than waiting to be overtaken by events. Stay in control. Why trust to luck when you can trust yourself? Be smart! Move early and do it in style.

Kendal Reporter, January 13, 2009
FURTHER THOUGHTS FROM CUMBERLAND

So, you have taken the good advice to move to Cumberland before it was absolutely necessary and made your move. What's next? You will find, as I did, that someone comes around three times a day for the first three days to "take your vital signs." That's to establish a baseline. Smile and cooperate; this too shall pass. Thereafter, a nurse will want to weigh you and take your blood pressure once a week.

You will discover a fridge, microwave and toaster oven across from the Cumberland dining room. These are yours to command. The Cumberland lounge boasts two daily papers, a TV, card tables, easy chairs, a full kitchen and access to a lovely garden.

Residents who need help with their medications get them in the lounge, or you can keep them in a locked box. A schedule of daily programs and entertainments is posted in the lounge and you can attend if that is your pleasure, but no one will urge you to do so. Ditto with respect to pushing wheel chairs. They check four times a night to be sure you have not fallen and are lying helpless on the floor, but you can sign a waiver and this will be reduced to once a night at 11:30 when the shift changes.

Welcome to assisted living. It's part of the cocoon of well-being that billions of people our age the world over envy and wish they had. Enjoy it.

Creative Lives

Listening to one another's stories invariably induced strong feelings; there were wet eyes in the room every time we met. We heard each other's stories about childhood abuse, fleeing the Holocaust, visiting eccentric relatives, or enjoying a special place. I discovered that the class was a safe environment in which to express the feelings and emotions inherent in the story I was telling. I was developing a new voice; one that could face and express feelings that had long been buried.

— ERNEST KIMMEL

Finding a New Voice

Ernest Kimmel

Much of my working life was spent writing, and sometimes speaking. When I arrived at Kendal, I considered myself quite adept at writing. I had generated scores of the proposals, reports, and memoranda that clog the arteries of any "modern" organization. I had also authored many papers, chapters, books, and other publications that represent "productivity" in the professional academic milieu. Because I worked in a context that highly valued verbal communication, much of my writing had been reviewed and edited by people who were considered professional writers and "communicators." I had learned much about writing from the comments of these professionals.

At one period of my life, I was frequently called on to meet with journalists and other scoundrels who were determined to challenge the practices of the organization for which I worked. To improve my skills at talking without saying anything, I was sent for several days to a firm called *Communispond* where I was coached in the art of persistently making "my" points, that is, not answering the question that was asked but rather the question I preferred to answer.

All in all, I knew that I had developed considerable skill in writing and talking over the almost 60 years since I was a tongue-tied, typewriter- blocked freshman who was shocked to receive a D- on the first couple of assignments in General Education A (a fancy name for freshman English). Yet my first year at Kendal revealed a large gap in my skills of communication; I had no experience in communicating feelings and emotions!

I got the first inklings of this communications gap when I began to participate in The Playreaders' monthly reading of one or two plays. Prior to Kendal, I had enjoyed watching dramas but had not participated in such an enterprise since a Christmas pageant when I was a schoolboy. Assuming the persona of a character, even for a few minutes, meant that I had to think about the character's emotions and the way in which they were expressed. I found that I enjoyed giving expression to the variety of emotions issuing from whatever character I was assigned to read.

Such vicarious expression of feelings and emotions had to be transformed into personal expressions of feelings and emotions as I began to participate in a memoir-writing course a few months after arriving at Kendal. My initial efforts were in my well-crafted, non-affective, prose —and were as dull as the proverbial dishwater. Prof. Brick, our patient teacher, kept nudging me to dig deeper into my memories of the events about which I was writing and to recover my sensations, feelings, and reactions. I found this very difficult since, as I was discovering, I had never been encouraged to express emotions either orally or in writing. My parents kept a tight rein on the expression of their emotions and, as a child, I learned to "make nice" and not give voice to what I was feeling. Most of my school teachers rewarded the use of language to convey information and ideas, not to express feelings—be it pleasure, anger, embarrassment, or sorrow. My mother always modeled staying calm and unemotional, even at the times of her parents' deaths. There was always the implied hint that it was a sign of weakness to show emotion.

One of the key features of the memoir-writing course was to read aloud the two or three page "memoir" we had written in the past few days. Listening to one another's stories invariably induced strong feelings; there were wet eyes in the room every time we met. We heard each other's stories about childhood abuse, fleeing the Holocaust, visiting eccentric relatives, or enjoying a special place. I discovered that the class was a safe environment in which to express the feelings and emotions inherent in the story I was telling. I was developing a new voice; one that could face and express feelings that had long been buried.

Over the past two years I have continued to remember past experiences along with the emotions associated with those experiences. It is very easy for me to lapse into the non-expressive, passive voice that I used for so many decades, but friends and family have encouraged me when I have used my new voice to express a different level of experience.

In particular, the use of this new voice has enabled me and a dear friend to open a dialogue about our early lives, sharing with each other feelings about our natal families that we had not previously dared to express to each other during the six decades of our friendship. As we have exchanged things we have written and as we've been able to discuss those when together, we both have grown. The accepting, nurturing community of Kendal has, indeed, opened opportunities to learn to express myself as well as to understand myself.

Shakespeare at Kendal
Allan Brick

Shakespeare preceded me as a full-time resident at Kendal. He came in many forms, but they all added up to Jack Shepherd. Jack was a former actor, indeed a British actor. Some decades earlier, Jack had come to the U.S. with his American wife, Janet. Both were Quakers, and together they had led settlement houses and youth programs. One of his specialties had been what he called Five Minute Shakespeare. He had developed this form in London and he said it transported well. He said that on the street you could hold people's attention for up to five minutes, but after that you would lose them.

Jack's principal cause in life was to bring great theatre to the people, so he wrote miniature versions of the great plays: Five-minute Hamlet, Five-minute Julius Caesar, Five-minute Othello, and so forth. Even though Shakespeare had taken up to three hours, it required only five minutes to show Hamlet taking bloody revenge upon his uncle for killing his father, his mother having been a sexual pawn. Similarly, in five minutes, Brutus and his gang could dispatch Caesar and get his own comeuppance, and Othello could be sent in to such a frenzy of race-based jealousy that he strangled his beloved white wife, only to discover that he'd been wrong about her. Jack had taken these five-minute Shakespeare works from the streets to the radio, where Philadelphia audiences heard them rendered by passionate young people, Jack himself filling in with narration and bit parts.

Before coming to America, Jack had a career on the British stage, in community theatre as well as London productions. He delighted to tell of occasions when he had been on the

same stages as Gielgud and Olivier. Even though Jack continued to be fundamentally Church of England, he came to live
at Kendal with his Quaker wife Janet, having himself become a Friend some decades before. At Sunday meeting for
worship attendees enjoyed Jack's rendering of the Biblical
quotations and stories he had learned in his early life attend-
ing regular services in his London "public school."

At Kendal he achieved what every actor desires and
seldom achieves: a long run. He was always in performance
as an actor or as producer-director. He was particularly
notable as organizer of monthly resident readings of
Shakespeare plays. He believed that everyone needed to act
in Shakespeare and develop accordingly. Fifteen to twenty
of us, depending on who could make it, gathered in a conference room. In Jack's and his Bard's hands it was an inspired
group; but unlike the Bard himself, no one lived forever.

Jack led us through the plays, the comedies, tragedies,
and his favorite history plays, one or two acts a time. He
assigned parts. We would all want the juicy ones. Indeed,
once I got to be Richard III, once Enobarbus, and once I was
the Duke making gorgeously poetic love to Olivia. I
was very good at these, and like most of us did some rehearsing ahead of time.

Being good at them or well cast, however, wasn't the
point. Jack was carefully democratic in his assigning. So I
never got Mark Anthony in *Julius Caesar*; the person who
did botched it badly—bad eyes—and I shuddered as Jack,
with infinite patience, kept him on track. He taught us all
how there was that of the worthy actor in every person,
just as George Fox would have recognized. So whether it
was King Hamlet's ghost or even Bottom in *Midsummer
Night's Dream*, we poured ourselves into it, heart and soul.

Once, for just one act and one session, I was Romeo. Not
only that, I played opposite the greatest Juliet I have ever
known. Ada was a frail resident in her early 90's who lived

in an assisted living apartment and needed a wheelchair. She herself or, later, an attendant wheeled her in to every one of Jack's Shakespeare sessions. She was a natural-born actress. Normally her voice seemed as frail as she was, but when she read a part, it was fully mellifluous, and her diction and pace was a marvel. I admit that I closed my eyes then to have this gorgeously passionate young Juliet speak to me.

Jack did cheat a little on his democratic casting principle when it came to Ada —for as I recall she also read Olivia, and oh, so memorably, Cleopatra. Her transition from the pure and innocent Juliet to the overpoweringly seductive Queen of Egypt was a director's dream. Yes, Jack cheated a bit on his democratic casting principle; I am forever deeply grateful that he had Ada as Portia convincing us that "the quality of mercy is not strained, / but droppeth like the gentle dew from heaven."

As a prelude to each of these sessions Jack talked about an experience on the British stage, often from a touring production in community theatre. He was determined to bring us into a sense of what the theatre, Shakespeare in particular, meant in England, and what it still means for audiences here and could mean for audiences everywhere.

British to the core, Jack ranked Charles Dickens right up there close below Shakespeare. He could pick up on almost any Dickens character and bring it to life. He could render a living Micawber, an outrageous Fagin, an irrepressible Sary Gamp, or the escaped convict Magwitch who introduced himself to Pip by holding him upside down in that graveyard.

Then there was Jack's Scrooge. On the Saturday evening before every Thanksgiving he read *A Christmas Carol* to a packed auditorium of residents and invited guests. The first of these performances I attended made me long for the next, the next, and the next. No one wanted to miss what might be, and what finally was the last one. He read from his own cut version, for he knew not to demand more than an hour from this particular audience, even though many of us wanted more.

This Christmas-time production harked back to Dickens' own style in his own public performances. Jack's wife Janet set the stage with a reading desk, a rug, and a Victorian-looking lamp. At the moment of pending performance she would straighten his jacket and brush up his hair and would wheel him up the ramp onto the low platform stage that had audience on three sides; he would come into the light, looking quizzically alert with his scarf flamboyant. Sitting at the reading desk he would nod to us, arrange his spectacles, and his marvel of a British actor's voice would begin. Each of us was held in thrall right down to Tiny Tim's "God bless us every one." He would end in tears—real tears, though of course he was aware of their performance value. I was in tears too, not wiping them off, but grateful every time. There would be a hush. Then came our applause and ovations and the perilous moment when some in wheelchairs risked standing up with the rest.

In those final Dickens years Jack was in an electric wheelchair touring the halls, pausing to greet each of us, his friends, his students, his Shakespeare tribe. Life continued as an exhilarating performance. He would stop with each person he met and you would pause with him. He would ask how you were, what you were reading, and, if he guessed that you had yourself been on a recent theatre trip, what was the play and how was the production. He would pick up on something you said, and, listening intently, he would give your words back to you, making them unique. Often this would lead him to an anecdote from his life on the stage or an experience with a kid on the street, or even to some bit of a Biblical story that he remembered his headmaster delivering to assembled students. You wanted to keep standing there listening, feeling honored, important.

The Human Figure and Its Passions
Laura Pizzuto-Velaz

As I look around my small Kendal studio, I realize my work from the beginning of my professional life has been about the human figure and its passions. Much emotion is revealed in these images, from my drawing of an infant implying the rapid movement of arms and legs to the male and female figures moving together across a yellow field. These nude paintings, about paint, color, and the viscous sensuality of human skin, show my quest over the years to improvise with sureness in whatever media I find useful.

My *Lip-Landscapes* give the impression that a person is behind the images, thinking, daydreaming, or recalling an incident. They are painted fantasies that can be read and ruminated upon like stories. What are they doing? Why are they there? How does the color tell you what it's about? There is passion in the paint. It's my way of telling the internal strivings we all live with.

The *Kissing Couple* is also about dancing, with an echo of them in the green field beyond. This is about love, and its expression in pink and redness is caught up in a cool, green landscape. Red lines define and hug the space that nourishes them. Brushstrokes, active and demanding, splash the surfaces.

Then one day, I injured my right thumb. Immediately, I called the left hand to duty. Amazingly, I discovered it was ready with a new expression in style. This was both mysterious and useful. My right brain took over and I was thrilled with the unanticipated change in my work. However, it took about six months before my left hand was skilled enough for me to really control its movement, giving me two expressions of the figure. With the right hand I could use charcoal to give a painterly definition and with the left had I produced a single line of clear, open space levity.

Two other problems have challenged me as a figure artist at Kendal. It's difficult to hire a model and it's difficult to find an appropriate place to work. I've not solved the problem, but hope to figure it out. No pun intended.

NUDES IN THE DINING ROOM
Allan Brick

Laurie's Pizzuto's reflections on her work remind me of how her nudes created a controversy and demonstrates how Kendal solves problems. There's a wall in our dining room reserved for the works of particularly accomplished artists. When Laurie displayed her paintings there, two of the eight were nudes. Thus, Laurie had created a rumble that became an aesthetic controversy. These two paintings celebrated the human form. One showed the nude impressionistically, verging on the abstract. The other showed a beautiful male body.

A photo of the critic who began the protest would have shown a woman sitting at a table immediately in of front of the nude, fork raised to her mouth as she struggled to eat her dinner. It would have revealed her outrage at having to view this nude as she ate. She protested.

Forces rallied on both sides. Defenders of free expression and modern cultural awareness sprang to the fore. They asked, "Had Laurie's exhibitions at a number of art galleries ever caused such excitement?" People coming for dinner would, first thing, go and take a look. When the dining room closed, people went through a back entrance to see. A pro-art high school waitress became the star idealistic and outspoken in her support of Laurie's paintings, she herself was a beautiful woman who embodied the very form that had been so upsetting.

Finally, into our open mail boxes came a letter from Ed Brubaker, a retired Presbyterian clergyman and former president of the Kendal Residents Association, that settled it. With his accustomed eloquence, Ed noted the community's responsibility for artistic freedom. He made it clear that it was Kendal's good fortune to have serious painters living here. So Miltonesque was this statement that it not only quashed all protest but it allowed residents to recognize how fortunate they were to have had the controversy.

How sad it would have been if that critic had not come to dinner that night. The community would have lost this opportunity to reflect upon the interdependence of art and freedom.

A Half Day in the Life of Joan
Joan Stemmler

I, Joan, age 80 plus, have lived here with my husband Ed exactly two years in one of the new cottages at Kendal. What is one of my mornings like? I hope you may wonder and keep on reading.

Yesterday, I had a class to go to. I try to rise at least two hours before the appointed time so I won't be late. Tardiness is a failing of mine. So is another one of not checking the location of meetings. This Wednesday I was on top of my game. Breakfast and morning chores finished by nine, I was well on my way to actually arriving early!

Allan Brick is a resident here. His literature class is considering the topic of Being Old: Part II. I missed Part I last year, being new, but I have learned not to miss whatever Allan has to offer. The first two books of the year, by Vita Sackville-West and Kasuo Ishiguro, led to so much of interest that I couldn't wait for the discussion of Penelope Lively's *Moon Tiger*. Since I arrived at the first class in September—a day late and just made it on the stroke of 10:15 for the second, I was confident that I might even be among the earliest to arrive this time.

Book and notes in my folder, hearing aids in my ears, eyeglasses on my nose, name tag on my right shoulder, destination Wellness Center Second Floor in my head, smart phone in my purse. Check. Hand on my door-knob and foot out the door, I heard the telephone ring.

I would deal with it quickly.

This was not to be. The call was from the widow of one of my husband's early colleagues. Two sentences into the conversation, I realized I was speaking with someone who was in a stage of memory loss. And how did I recognize this? Here at Kendal we are deeply dedicated to education about issues of old age. A member of our administration had organized the previous evening's program featuring an outside speaker. Teepa Snow led us towards knowledge about Alzheimer's and other dementias that over half of us may face as we age. We were encouraged as a whole community to learn methods to help us wisely live with and help those afflicted with these diseases. We may in time be them ourselves.

So I tried to practice what I learned with my old acquaintance of many years. And indeed I was able communicate to her that my husband would call her when he got home.

But, to continue my particular elderly saga, I belatedly walked out the door and started up toward the correct location at top speed. I crossed the road without really looking to my left. A movement caught my eye. A slowly approaching ecologically correct hybrid car was obeying the 20 mph speed limit. It had noiselessly stopped to allow me to get to the other side. I saw who it was. Oh no. Our empathetic head of social work. She saw my careless move. Just the other day she had noticed me in one of the hallways looking puzzled and kindly inquired if I was lost. Oh no! She's going to think I'm losing it. But I exercised that other gift of mine, that of laughing at myself. I was in a good humor when I reached the correct place just in time.

The presentation and discussion of Penelope Lively's book were stimulating and thought provoking. One of our participating residents had spent time in Egypt. She described in detail the workings of the spiral coil of the device with the trade name Moon Tiger. When the end of the coil is lit, its pyrethrum laden fumes serve to keep deadly malaria carrying mosquitoes away from the sleeping inhabitants of a room throughout the night. Allan wrapped up with a discussion of the central motif of the spiral and of Lively's skill in weaving together her extraordinary novel of love and death.

I hope this excerpt from my experience opens a window letting you have a glimpse into "my" Kendal. We all know about the journey ahead for us, whatever our role shall be. I for one am glad to be making that journey in this place devoted to growing in understanding, in compassion and in friendship.

First Saturday

Marjean Willett

I wake about seven, as I do every day. The coffee pot is ready, I just tap the button and it starts to gurgle. Soon I'm sitting in the rocking chair, sipping and reading the *New York Times* on my IPad. I'd rather read a real newspaper, but I can't seem to get it delivered before 8:30. I like to read it between seven and eight, a habit I got into when my late husband was not well, and I needed that quiet hour before he got up. From the rocking chair I can see the bright zinnias in my garden in the summer.

In the winter I just enjoy the wall I face, which is painted a bright coral. Usually I eat breakfast at home, at my kitchen table, with a double-crostic puzzle to keep me company. But it's Saturday, and at 8:25 I head for the Coffee Shop where I will join the Unitarian Table. Recently when I told someone I was a lapsed Unitarian, they said "How lapsed can you get?" Actually, the liberal Democratic Table would be a more appropriate title. Our table got smaller during the last year, as three members died. We are now five: Penny and Laurie from Cumberland, Jan, Marilyn, and myself from the cottages. When I first wrote this paragraph, we were six. But on a recent Saturday Wiltrude was missing. We found that she had gone to the hospital, and on Sunday, sadly, she died.

I splurge and usually have a large pancake and one sausage. I'll have my orange juice later at home, with my pills. I don't like Kendal orange juice. Others like the Kendal oatmeal, but I can eat that at home. I've tried the scrambled eggs, but I'm fussy about those, too. While we eat, we may talk about the weather or the world. Marilyn says "My dog hates that thunder!" She is also the expert on the Saturday night movie, because she's on the film committee.

When the table first started, years ago, I started bringing in Tony Auth cartoons, because I was the only one taking the *Philadelphia Inquirer*. As a newcomer to the area, I thought I should take the local paper, but it began to shrink, so I switched to the *Times*. But the cartoon habit continues, and I now print out eight from the *Washington Post* website. Tony Auth was still there until he died recently, along with Tom Toles, Pat Oliphant, Ben Sargent, Nick Anderson, Stuart Carlson and Mike Luckovich. We pass them around and it leads to discussion. Of course, we have time for a little gossip, too. Later, the cartoons go on to Kay, then to Emil, where they are picked up by Eliza.

After breakfast, I head for the indoor pool. I like the therapy pool, since I exercise rather than swim, and the slightly warmer temperature is nice. I have a routine that lasts exactly one half hour. I may have it all to myself, or share it with Barbarajene. A few minutes in the hot tub is a wonderful way to combat the aches and pains of old age. Mary often comes just as I leave.

Slightly exhausted, I head for home which is about a five minute walk, although it seems to get longer and longer as I get older. But a spell in that rocking chair and all is well. I may finish reading today's paper, or start on the sections of the real Sunday paper that are delivered on Saturday. By taking the Sunday paper, I get the rest of the week free digitally. Funny, I like to read the real paper in my wing chair. I suppose it's because the light is better, coming in over my left shoulder. I don't need as much light with the IPad, which has its own, and it sits better on my lap in the rocking chair.

After the paper reading, I have lunch in the kitchen.

Maybe peanut butter on whole grain bread, with some bread-and-butter pickle slices added. A few mini carrots or a tomato salad and some fruit and I'm done. After lunch I check my E-mails and fight off the desire for a nap. I'll do some grocery shopping, read a book, or pay some bills. If I get exhausted from all that I'll sink back into the rocking chair and play solitaire or Scrabble on my IPad.

But by late afternoon, it's time to change for dinner at 5:30. It's the first Saturday of the month, and I have a special table tonight. It was started by Ruth McMurry who is no longer with us, but whom we remember fondly each month. It now also includes Ellie, Merritt, Violet, Harry, Melody, Peter, Vi, and Will. Ruth always had *New Yorker* cartoons for place cards, but Merritt has made us permanent ones with a suitable sketch for each. Mine has a palette, Violet's some music. It's an interesting group and the conversation is never dull. It's often pretty funny, too. Peter can be counted on for some laughs. Violet's exuberant laughter makes us all laugh harder. Her answering-machine message is just her laughing.

After dinner, we usually head for the auditorium, where we may have Pre-Kendal Memories, one of the most popular programs at Kendal, an offering from the Saturday Night Live committee, or a movie. And so ends my First Saturday. Life at Kendal is not boring.

Jo Mullen, Kendal Artist

Peggy Gwynn

In her Westmorland room
She sat painting, at an easel
I paused at her doorway.
A nurse, in passing, whispered,
"That's Jo Mullen, an artist

Still painting—though she's blind."
I found "Josephine Mullen"
in *Who's Here at Kendal.*
It told me she had studied
At the Art Students League
In New York City. Now,
I really planned to visit her.

•

She told me, "Yes, I paint…
and I can't really see.
Only in my mind's eye.
A friend sets the canvas up,
Stretched to the size I ask for,
the brush and the colors I need.

"I do mostly abstracts,
And can pretty well tell
where the brush strokes should go.
Been painting most all
my life. It's experience
that guides my hand, I guess."

•

The paintings on her wall
and propped here and there
I thought beautifully accomplished.
Some hang in Kendal hallways.
I asked if I could buy one
and was told they're not for sale.

The Quilt

Marjean Willett

I'm thinking of quilts
And I'm thinking of Kendal
And I think that Kendal
Is like a great sprawling quilt—
A quilt whose patterns
And colors are always changing.

Bright Hopes

I'm thinking of quilt patterns
And I remember the founders
Whose "Bright Hopes" and
"Strength in Union" made
Kendal a reality.

Strength in Union

And I think that the pieces change
But the patterns persist—
"Carpenters Square" and
"Flight of Swallows" and
Of course "Tree Everlasting."

Carpenters Square

The pieces are you and me,
And they are dark and light,
Bright and dull, plain and
Fancy. Each new piece
Changes the quilt a little
But the whole stays strong.

Flight of Swallows

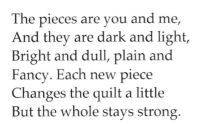

Tree Everlasting

It Happened Right Here!

The knob loosened, it wobbled, it collapsed, it fell apart. In those wonderful seconds as I lay propped in bed awaiting the dramatic moment when the door would burst open, the sign of absolute success, it occurred to me, yes, things do go wrong, and as usual, quite unexpectedly. But when, ever again, will I have two handsome men banging on the door to get into my bedroom? —BARBARA HALLOWELL

Maintenance Came on the Trot

Barbara Hallowell

Things go wrong—usually quite unexpectedly. One autumn night when I gleefully leapt into bed, propped myself against soft pillows and snuggled up with a good book, the world faded into blissful oblivion, a pleasure I anticipated almost daily, sensing it ever more acutely as the clock approaches the appropriate hour for me to retire.

All seemed perfect—except the ball game. Tom had TV football playing in the far room, thoughtfully lowered in volume but still loud enough that its distant goings-on and noisy enthusiasm distracted me. I bounced out of bed, gave the bedroom door a solid push, and—and it didn't go shut. I banged it again, it bounced back at me. I jiggled and twisted the knob, poked and pushed the latch. Them climaxing a truly hearty slam, it closed obediently, though with an un-usually determined click. Back to bed, book and bliss.

Eventually the husky, helmeted men who huddle and scurry about on the football field and fall down, only to repeat the whole sequence again, and then again and again, went to their locker rooms. Tom flipped off the TV and headed for bed, but the door into our bedroom refused to open. He jiggled, twisted, poked, pushed and banged while I sat in bed laughing, which was not helpful. The door refused to open. I tried it from my side, without success.

The situation lost its humor. I was locked in, Tom was locked out, the hour was late and that door stood resolutely between us. But there is joy in Kendal when such night time problems arise. Just call Westmorland, our nursing station. Westmorland pages Maintenance, and Maintenance comes on the trot. The young man who arrived jiggled, twisted, poked, and pushed and banged, but the door continued obstinate.

I heard a low conversation followed by a sound of a different nature. Apparently a tool was working on the door's Achilles heel, a tiny peg in the knob assembly. The knob loosened, it wobbled, it collapsed, it fell apart.

In those wonderful seconds as I lay propped in bed awaiting the dramatic moment when the door would burst open, the sign of absolute success, it occurred to me, yes, things do go wrong, and as usual, quite unexpectedly. But when, ever again, will I have two handsome men banging on the door to get into my bedroom?

A 4:45 Confessional
Vi Luginbuhl

Prior to coming to Kendal, we had heard about the famous 4:45 but knew very little about what to expect. What do you wear? Do you bring a gift to the hostess? Are you expected to bring your own wine? Do you write thank you notes? Was a 4:45 like a large, neighborhood cocktail party at which everyone is talking, the noise level is unbearable and laryngitis is threatening? Are new people carefully analyzed to find out if they "fit in?" Are there little cliques of individuals who tend to exclude? Do residents gossip about each other?

All of these questions went through my mind after we arrived. However, one I didn't think of but later confronted was how to recover from forgetting an invitation.

One evening very soon after our arrival, we were enjoying a glass of wine with the Whitlocks, who lived across the walkway. Ian and Marianne were describing the many activities offered here at Kendal when the telephone interrupted the conversation.

Fran Gilbert on the line inquired," Did you remember that you were to be here for a 4:45 this evening?"

I did not remember and responded, "Fran, you must be mistaken. It is not on my calendar." She reminded me that we had arranged an earlier 4:45, then cancelled and rescheduled. "Yes," I remembered, "but it is on my calendar for next week." Clearly, I had penciled in the wrong week. Not knowing Fran or anyone else very well, I was terribly embarrassed and sorry. Although the Gilberts were most gracious, I continued to brood about making such a social faux pas.

All of those earlier anxieties about Kendal's 4:45s were quickly put to rest, and it soon became apparent that forgetting about an invitation was not so unusual. More than once I have seen the hostess look at her watch and with a twinkle in her eye, say "John must have forgotten, I'll call him." John arrives a little late and with a quick apology settles in for another pleasant 4:45. Although I realized that it was not such an uncommon event, I remained cross with myself and was still brooding about my own forgotten invitation almost a year later.

After we moved to the new cottage at the other end of campus, I saw Fran in the hall at the Center one day and invited her and Dave for a 4:45 the following week. Unfortunately, by the time I finished my errands, I forgot that I had invited them and of course neither put it on the calendar nor mentioned it to Will. In the meantime, we set up a 4:45 with two other couples for that evening.

I don't remember who else came, but six of us were engaged in conversation when Dave and Fran came to the door. The minute I saw them, I remembered that hallway invitation, and was happy to include them. My efforts to pretend that I was expecting them, however, could hardly have been convincing. They could clearly view only six seats, six coasters, six napkins and six hors d'oeuvres plates. Trying desperately not to appear nonplussed, I pulled up two chairs and added the necessaries for drinks and finger food. Will took Fran's drink order and hustled Dave into the kitchen. Both drink Manhattans, but each like a different recipe, so Dave fixed his own. Will gave Fran her drink and returned to the kitchen with Dave to be sure he found all the proper ingredients for his drink, I supposed. They talked quietly for a time before joining the rest of us.

The living room conversation grew lively enough that I could slip off to the bedroom and call the dining room to increase our table reservation to eight. Having finished that detail, I mumbled to myself. "Maybe, I pulled this off."

The evening went well, I thought, and it was only on the way back to the cottage after dinner that I learned about Will's conversation with Dave over Manhattans. Typically to the point Will asked, "Are you sure you came to the right house tonight?"

I felt a vice gripping my viscera. After all my efforts to pretend, I was exposed! "Why did you ask him that?" I wailed. All my old humiliation about forgetting returned with a vengeance and I kept asking myself why both times with the Gilberts?

I believe I have been forgiven, at least I sincerely hope so. Time is a great healer, and now I am amused not pained. It has taken almost three years for me to understand that forgetting isn't an affront to the inviter. It happens here at Kendal. We understand and pretending otherwise isn't necessary.

Two Community Vignettes
Trudy Huntington

Where Are We Going?
I was visiting in the nursing section when I heard footsteps in the hall and an obviously elderly voice asked, "Where are we going?"

"To your bath," was the cheerful answer.

"I don't want to bathe."

"Bathing feels good."

"I am old enough to know what I want. I do *not* want to bathe," said in a very determined voice.

"Would you like a shower?" was the sweet answer

"What is a shower?"

"A shower is like standing in the rain, warm rain."

"All right, I'll have a shower."By this time they were down the hall and out of earshot.

HELP! More Scotch Tape, please!
The community office room, open for anyone's use, is planned and equipped the by the residents. There is an excellent copy machine that one pays for on the honor system, There is a typewriter and dictionary, a large paper cutter, several hole punchers of different sizes, numerous pencils and paper clips, various staplers and a large roll of scotch tape.

One day I noticed that the tape dispenser was empty— I was in a hurry and gave it little thought. The next day there was a sign taped to the dispenser. In large letters, in red ink, was written, "HELP! More Scotch Tape Please"

Nothing happened for several days. Then there appeared on the bottom of the sign, written in small letters, in black ink, *To see the need is to volunteer.*" A few days later there was a fresh roll of tape.

Kendal's Perle Mesta
Cynthia Kuespert

Shortly before we moved into one of the new, spacious cottages at Kendal, we'd been forewarned about the rather quaint tradition of "4:45s." But I'm not sure we were prepared for the first invitation we received from the Perle Mesta of Kendal, the elegant 93 year-old Ruth McMurry. My appointed seat was marked by a place card, a cartoon from the *New Yorker* magazine, showing a woman looking around a cavernous room, similar to an art museum, and asking her husband, "Do you think we'll have room for all our paintings?" Yes, it was a little dig at the new cottage residents and an expression of some legitimate apprehension of those wondering how these new space-hungry aliens would fit into Kendal.

After a good laugh, at our expense, the conversation quickly turned to opinions about the new Barnes Museum, and then to a debate about the role of the U.S. in Iraq and finally to the adaptation of species in South America. To begin the evening with a good natured ice-breaker and end with a discussion of Darwin elevated our opinion of 4:45s, not just a "quaint," but possibly a "curious" tradition of hospitality.

I think Don was still comparing notes with someone on Gurdjieff when I went home, checked to make sure our subscription to the *New York Times* was current, and ordered three years of the *New Yorker*.

The Drama Club
Fran Gilbert

Claire leaves her scooter on the front porch of the clubhouse, and carefully steps through the hall to the meeting room, holding on to each piece of furniture she passes. Louisa is wearing, as usual, her Yankees hat, to cover her lack of hair due to radiation—a breast removed.

It's a nice day, but many have jackets on. As we grow older, we grow cooler! John has his jacket on upside down. The collar is at hip level, the draw-string bottom over his shoulders. But oh! He is a mean Julius Caesar when we read Shakespeare. Andy sits by a lamp near a window. Light is everything to him as his eyes grow dim.

What's the play today? Doesn't matter; parts have been assigned in advance to some. Others are listeners. The classics, comedy, mysteries, modern plays are read. George Bernard Shaw to Garson Kanin. Tom Stoppard to Agatha Christie. All members of the cast are sitting down. There are no entrances and exits to master; no cues to pick up. No memorizing lines. The group gets started.

There is a slight shuffling of feet, and Fred rises and

leaves the room. That damned prostate! Act one, scene two. The laughter begins. This is a comedy. A line is said. The next line is Helen's. Helen? Aren't you "Amanda" in Scene two? A little nudge on Helen's arm from Rosa. Helen seems to be dozing.

A tiny "ping" sounds. Larry needs to test his blood sugar. Eats a graham cracker after. On with the reading. The play ends with a scene of riotous total confusion. It has been a thoroughly enjoyable session, and the decision is made that the Drama Club will read it in the auditorium soon.

Two weeks later, on a Saturday night, the play is *You Can't Take It with You*, and the audience is the entire Kendal community. There are many roles, and for some of these, the length between lines is long. A very funny play, and the actors are inspired by the laughter of the audience.

Some find the play most restful and relaxing, and a few may even fall asleep. A gentle snore now and then does not disturb those who do stay awake.

The cast, however, should always be on its toes. But during *You Can't Take It with You*, when it came time for Nan to say her lines, there was dead silence. Nan had fallen asleep!

Phone Calls from the Void
Gabrielle Griswold

When you move, you never know what unforeseen oddities may ensue. Sometimes none do, and sometimes well.... My own move to Kendal from New Hampshire was efficient, my settling in comfortable and quick, my feeling at home here virtually instantaneous. I began by learning faces, then first names, last names only last (and some I still don't know, as new residents keep coming!) My mail soon arrived in good order at the new address, so did my telephone calls at the new number. No oddities in the early days, and none immediately thereafter. At least, not for a while… .

Then, in slow increments, there began the intrusion into my life of a mysterious shadow figure. But who? Someone, apparently, whose former Pennsylvania telephone number *had now become mine*… . Some fellow, apparently, whom a lot of people have been seeking for at least eight years—as long as I've lived here… .

Although I know his name, I know nothing else about this penumbral person. He could be anyone. A mystery to me, he's just a man for whom the telephone calls keep coming. *And* coming—calls live and automated, in both male and female voices, while time and again I vainly attempt to convince them that *NO* Harry Alexander lives here, and *NO*, this is *NOT* his phone number… .

No, I explain to the live callers, *no!* There is no Harry Alexander here. If this telephone number ever was his, it no longer is because it's been *mine* now for *eight*—got that?— *EIGHT* whole years! And *no*, I do not know, have *never* known, anyone named Harry Alexander. "I cannot help you," I tell them firmly, "and I'd appreciate it if you would stop calling me. You're wasting my time and your own. Please *END* this—I do not wish to hear from you again."

"Thank you," the live callers indifferently drawl, and ring off. Until the next time… .

"This telephone call is for [*voice-over:* Har-ry Al-ex-an-der]" growl the solemn automated messages. "It is ve-ry im-por-tant that we contact [*voice-over:* Har-ry Al-ex-an-der] as soon as possible. If you are [*voice-over:* Har-ry Al-ex-an-der], please press One. If you would like us to call back later, press Two. To repeat this message, press Three. If you are *not* [*voice-*

over: Har-ry Al-ex-an-der], press Four." Exhilarated by this chance to interject my own reality, I hastily press four. "We are sor-ry for the in-con-ven-ience," rasps the automated voice, and the line goes dead. Until the next time… .

Meanwhile, I try to picture the scenario. Harry Alexander is a big-time scam artist who has conned zillions of people worldwide and Interpol are trying to track him down. *Or,* Harry Alexander is a slippery local scum-bag who skipped town years ago, leaving behind a pile of unpaid bills so vast that his banks and creditors are still hot to catch him. *Or,* he is a deadbeat dad who kidnapped his two kids, then disappeared off the map, leaving his frantic wife with neither children nor alimony… .

Or—more cheerfully—Harry Alexander is a hobo, who, as the last surviving member of his clan, has unknowingly fallen heir to a sizeable fortune. While he continues to sleep on park benches and feed at soup kitchens, his family's lawyers scour the country for him. *Or,* by some unimaginable fluke, he has won the lottery, inherited a race horse, or an English earldom—or been designated the Handsomest Homeless Man in America by some screwball poll, with a reward pending of ten thousand dollars… .

While the quest for Harry Alexander continues and I fume at this succession of pointless repeated phone calls, some tantalizing high drama is unfolding out there that I can only guess at. Who *is* Harry Alexander? Which one of his many aliases is that? And who are his pursuers? To this teasing tale, there is no satisfactory dénouement. As I vainly try to imagine what instigates these calls, I also wonder which is more frustrating: the persistent calls themselves— or my own persistent never-to-be-fulfilled curiosity as to what real-life story lies behind them… .

Meanwhile—since I have not the slightest intention of leaving Kendal—must I then just accept this shadow man as some sort of elusive phantom *roommate*…?

Undercover Surprise
Dorie Brubaker

One thing leads to another at Kendal, as well as through-out one's life. This story started when I decided my soprano efforts were no longer helpful in the Kendal Singers. Maybe, I thought, volunteering in Westmorland would be more helpful and fun. When I consulted Jan Clodius, Activities Director, she asked if I would be interested in reading to one or more residents living in our Health Center. That appealed to me. Soon I was reading to three very different and interesting people. Here's my story about one of these special Westmorland women.

When I first met her, she was lying down, full length, long and straight, under the covers. She was quiet but was interested as I read James Herriot's book *The Lord God Made Them All*. Herriot was a Yorkshire veterinarian who worked among the blunt-spoken farmers scattered in the North York-shire Hills, caring for their four legged patients when ail-ing or ill.

Week after week this woman listened, all laid out eyes closed, never stirring. Of course I wondered if she was in nod-off-land or with the vet in the Yorkshire Hills, but when I said, "Well, I'll be back next week and we can hear another chapter," the voice from the bed demanded, "Read another chapter," which, of course, I did!

One time, at the end of our time together, I said, "Kendal is having a spelling bee next Saturday and I'm in it!" Suddenly, she opened her eyes, came to life, raised up in the bed and said in a clear, authoritative voice, "I want to be in it!"

I answered, "I'm sure they've selected all the spellers, but you can take my place!"

I think my response was based on two quick thoughts: she sounded so confident and sure and, what fun it would be for her and for me! I pushed her to the auditorium for the rehearsal. She listened to all the directions.

On Saturday, Ed and I developed a conflict and missed the spelling bee. But the next day I heard that "She spelled every word correctly and won the bee,"

From under the covers, you never know.

Modesty Panel
Patricia Hunt

We sat like a row of eight old crows on the cement bench at the end of the Kendal pool, turning our heads in unison, following our instructor's directions. The skirt on my neighbor's dark suit was floating around her, defying her efforts to hold it down.

"How come your suit stays down?"

"I don't have a skirt," I answered, "I have a modesty panel."

I'd been taking water exercise classes ever since the indoor pool opened seven years ago. At first, I wore my old colorful suits which had blessed many a week at the shore. The elastic had stretched to accommodate my increasing girth and the skirts drooped comfortably down my thighs.

They brought back happy memories of family holidays. In the Kendal pool, however, their flowing skirts hindered my movements and in the hot tub, the tops blew up like two beach balls above the water. It was time to buy a new suit.

I searched the local stores, tried on numerous glamorous suits, even a two piece, designed for svelte bodies. Finally, I gave up and turned to the Internet. With the help of my granddaughter, I finally found what I needed. It was not the Speedo designed for Olympic swimmers or the swim dress for ladies my age but a chlorine resistant suit with a modesty panel in front that satisfied my Victorian upbringing.

Now as I sit in the hot tub or on the bench with jets pounding my back, I can lean back and relax. Even the day care toddlers, sitting cross legged like colorful birds, waiting their turn to spring into the pool, don't laugh. No longer does my skirt bob above the water. This elderly swimmer can sink gratefully into the shadowy depths, only my white head showing, before tripping, dripping to the safety of my towel.

Witness for Peace: Rain or Shine
Joan H. Nicholson

In the fall of 2009, the U.S. government announced that a "surge" of 30,000 soldiers would join the 71,000 soldiers in Afghanistan in order to "achieve victory." Actually, the purpose was to ensure control of access to natural resources, because that country has a vast amount of natural gas, trillions of dollars worth of minerals and is a strategic region for future oil and gas pipelines. In response to the U.S. war plans, many thousands of people across the nation decided to hold peace demonstrations. One such witness was to take place on the Old Kennett Meeting House lawn by Route 1 near the Kendal entrance, where I vigil every weekday. I had always been happy to have company, but this time especially, I hoped others would join me. I had posted announcements, and the word spread.

The appointed day dawned under gray heavy-laden skies. As the hour for the event neared, the heavens opened and rain began to fall. Disappointed, I set the bag of posters from our weekly vigil in Kennett Square against the stone wall near the Meeting House. It seemed improbable that anyone would venture out into the steady downpour. Suddenly there appeared through the deluge, an umbrella, then another and another, held by people clad in raingear. And more kept arriving! The group included John and Fran Beer, who participated in our weekly vigil, Brad Angell, and many other Kendalites. Then Jean Barker and Joy, her Labrador, arrived to join us from Crosslands. Finally, 17 had arrived, defying the elements in order to declare that our nation should embrace peace instead of war. The knowledge that we were part of demonstrations taking place throughout the country was very encouraging.

The purpose of our vigil as we stood for an hour by the highway was to share our peace message with those passing by. Most were driving more slowly because of the rain and when they stopped for the red light, some took special note, curious about why we were there in the inclement weather.

That dark and dreary day had transformed into one of grace and light. It will remain indelible in my mind even as other memories fade and vanish over time.

Our Caring Community

The head nurse assured me that a double bed had been ordered for Dudley's room! Soon it was in place, and an eight-by-eleven bright orange DO NOT DISTURB *laminated sign was provided to hang on our closed door. How much those afternoon times together meant to us!* — ROSALIND CAMPBELL

How I Became Tanner's Mom
Marianne Whitlock

I had a special feeling about Althea Whyte. I was new at Kendal in 2009, and I put out the word that hanging out near my home was a cat that did not seem feral, but seemed to want a home. At the time I had Rani, a princess Siamese cat. She really wanted to be an only cat, or so I felt. Althea called me about my distress notice. She could not take another cat at the time, but she offered to help me get the cat into a box, and take it to a good shelter. I ended up not needing her help because another person wanted to adopt the stray. But I remembered Althea and her kind offer.

Later, Althea's husband, Doug, decided he needed skilled nursing care and moved to Westmorland. Althea and Doug wanted to get a dog, and they went to a shelter and got Tanner, a tan-colored terrier/shih tzu mix. When I first met Tanner, he was spending three nights a week in the Whyte apartment with Althea and four nights in Westmorland with Doug. I saw some of the logistics problems they had and teamed up with Althea and Doug, doing a daily walk with Tanner.

One Wednesday, as was our custom, I picked Tanner up at Althea's apartment, intending to drop him off with Doug later in the afternoon. That was the last time I picked up Tanner at Althea's. She had gone to play water volleyball, a sport she enjoyed very much. During the afternoon I learned that Althea had been taken from the pool by ambulance to the hospital. When Tanner and I arrived at Westmorland, Doug had just been informed that Althea had died in the ambulance. I put Tanner in Doug's lap, and he held him closely and cried into Tanner's neck.

After losing Althea, Doug started wondering if he was going to lose Tanner because the staff at Westmorland might think the responsibility was too much for him, with his unsteady gait and less-than-optimal balance. The staff did not recommend his giving up Tanner, but Doug himself began to realize he was having difficulty managing. He had some discussions with Jan Clodius, the activities director for Westmorland, about the situation.

One Friday evening Jan Clodius, Doug, and I had a meeting. Doug expressed what he felt, and I expressed what I felt. There were several staff people who were interested in adopting Tanner if Doug made that decision. The meeting ended with my saying I would take Tanner for the weekend and discuss the situation with my husband, Ian. Ian had wanted another dog ever since our border collie, Kali, died in 2006. It was I who had been saying that I didn't want the responsibility again. When I took Tanner home that night and asked Ian, he said "Yes" immediately.

Now I am Tanner's Mom. I think he is a very happy guy. He has lots of important business around our home, like hiding his bones, and then finding them again. He plays with other dogs in the Pennsbury township dog park across Route 1. He shows his love for us by racing around our home when we first come in and cuddling up to us when we read or watch a movie. If we go out and do not try to head in any particular direction, Tanner will lead us all the way to Doug's room where he snuggles up to Doug, showing his loyalty by licking Doug's face.

A Painting Duo

Laura Pizzuto-Velaz

I know how this happened, but I never expected it. Paintings in watercolor hung on every wall near her room in Westmorland, the nursing facility at Kendal. I observed them with delight. She understood how to push paint around to enclose images of the landscape that seeped out of her mind. Talent! Yes, indeed, and as I walked by them for many months, an understanding of her person grew within me. She had a curious mind. She had traveled. She had been around in life, married with two children. She loved movement. There was a sweep in the skies, and the motion of wind in her brushstrokes. She evoked the power of emotion as her hands stroked the paper with brush and color that spoke to the observer standing in front of each painting. Occasionally, a figure or two might appear. They were, however, mostly incidental.

One day I had lunch in the coffee shop with Jack and Janet Shepherd. Upon nearly saying goodbye, Janet saw a woman across the room with a friend. The next thing was Janet saying, "Laurie, you must meet Annie Peck... ."

I responded, "Oh, yes, she's the painter I most admire here at Kendal."

Janet and I walked over by the window, and there in her wheelchair was this soft, bent figure with tousled white hair, smiling with her eyes. We had a little talk. Her voice shaped into some clipped Scots humor which left me happy, and we planned to meet again.

And we did meet in the hall. Annie, with her walker, was returning to her room from the Cumberland diningroom. I called her name, and she remembered me.

"Annie, your paintings give these walls an experience as one walks by... ."

"Oh, thank you," she said. "I began to paint when I was an old lady! I saw others painting, and I knew I could do it even better!"

I loved her spunk.

Another day, I took a painting of mine, a Lip Landscape, to the Gathering Room. Annie was there with six or seven others in wheelchairs. When I asked a sleepy woman what she thought the painting might say to her, she answered, "Hello..." and fell asleep again.

Annie said, "That bird near the lips is a farm bird, and shouldn't be there!"

She was quiet for a moment, and then softly remarked, "Those lips are very sensitive."

Her intuitions came easily, and captured a painted moment. I knew we could talk together about working with painted images, and their meaning.

I was aware that Annie now slept most of every day. She was somewhat depressed, but I believed she was bored and experiencing much loss. She had not painted in about five years, and complained of constant fatigue. There was some dementia, but she remembered me every time we met, and she knew my name. So we gathered all of her materials: her old brushes (one with tape on the handle and she remarked, "You can do everything with this one!") a big card table, her large watercolor paper, several sizes of sketch books. I ordered a new paint box which, when she saw it, she immediately adored.

To get her involved, I asked if I could draw her portrait. She said yes, and with charcoal and paper I sat across from her at lunch. The black and white format, charcoal lines forming her face and shoulders, disturbed her. She became furious. "It's ugly, and I don't have a fat face!"

My interpreting the lines and grey masses didn't soothe her. Taking in a few more of her observations, I changed the subject and went home to my studio. There I finished the portrait. I returned to Annie's room the next day. She was sleepy, but we talked just the same. She recognized herself in the drawing and remarked, "My two eyes are different, aren't they?"

"Yes, Annie, they are, and I'm glad you saw that. Everyone has some asymmetry in their face." I realized that her vision was acute, and that she observed with feeling. This meant that we would be able to share a painting experience.

She didn't want to start. Crystal, her caretaker, said, "It's stimulation, Annie." I brought out the card table and set it up in front of her as she sat on the bed. The paper stored under her bed was easy to slip out and plunk down so she could choose the size. Too big was too much. She chose half size, and began two blue mountains, and a "loch." A generous start. Annie rather swept the brush over and over the image not to let it go. Or: where to go next? She had some difficulty seeing the colors, but I pointed and spoke them. Her tempo rose. A boathouse came next, and much self-criticism. We encouraged her efforts, especially after she called out, "What a thing to ask an old woman to do!"

"It's been a very long time since you last painted, Annie, and you will find your skills again. It will take some practice."

Annie rubbed her hands to feel them, and I took one and rubbed it to assure her that they were fine. She was concerned that mine were cold! Annie carried on with a boat, changing the color and size and making it more of a canoe. Sighing, she decided to stop working. Crystal then said that stimulation was good for her, and added that the painting was going well.

I suggested moving up to the sky, and she snapped, "If you want to paint, do your own. This is my painting. I don't need suggestions."

"Sure, Annie. Next time I'll paint across from you on the table. It'll be great."

Satisfied, she went on to develop trees at the bottom of the mountain. The whole painting was floating on the bottom edge of the paper. She fashioned another mountain, and spent the rest of the hour filling trees with branches. This was an impressive amount of time for a first visit with materials. Annie had had a bath, dressed, and now had painted for an hour and five minutes. It was a good, and a famous, start!

So we began. A few days of this were encouraging as she began to renew her skills. Over the following weeks she showed progress and even some satisfaction in the paintings she was producing.

Then the news was that Annie had had two small strokes. She remained one night in the hospital, and returned by ambulance the next morning. There was a period when one side of her face slumped, and the same side was weak down the rest of her body. When I saw her that morning, Beth was helping, and was urging her to eat. A bite of egg was all Annie would take. It was a good effort though. She was sitting up, an oxygen mask across her face as a bit of crystal deco-ration. Her mood was good as she announced that she was dying today. I assured her that this wasn't a good day for dying, and we yet had painting to do. She actually agreed with me! Her humor was still available. When I dropped in the next evening, Annie was accompanied by a new person sitting next to the window while Annie was lying down, covered and sleepy. She was less animated. It was hard to know how she felt at that moment, whether it was sleep or depression. Or both. She came to, and again announced that she was dying. I think she enjoyed saying that, and that it was still going on.

Some weeks later, after I had been away, I visited her. I approached her bed, where she was resting. There were two pairs of identical red shoes dropped on to the floor. It was a little as though she had been dancing and had left them waiting so she could resume. There dozing in her sweats, she looked very athletic.

After my bright hello she opened her eyes. She announced that she was doing poorly, and I told her how well she seemed. When I asked her about the red shoes, she remarked that it was allowed! Continuing on that subject, she repeated that she was a very, very old lady but she was going to dance, dance, dance until she died. I said, "Annie, will you paint until you die?"

"No, I have given that up...."

"Why, Annie? Your talent is still with you."

"No. What I would paint would look terrible." But she added, "Well, modern art being what it is, maybe that would be all right!"

"Yes, Annie. You can always develop whatever happens on the paper."

"It's possible. But I certainly don't want to do it today. I'm sorry."

"You mustn't be sorry. I'll come another day, when you are not so sleepy."

"Oh, thank you, Laurie. That would be good."

My next pop-in visit found Charlotte Osborne with Annie. They were looking at a book about Tuscany. The both had memories to share, and my memories came up too. We did some happy talking about long ago days in Europe, and Annie told a story about her husband, George. He was a Naval captain and a spy. In the story, he was hiking during the Second World War in the Alps to escape capture by the Germans. A mist and fog hid the group of soldiers as they approached the peak to protect them, but as soon as they had sopped down the other side the fog lifted completely and exposed them to the enemy. Annie laughed, saying that the German officers couldn't figure out why a naval officer was in the mountains at all. This was the most animated I had seen Annie in a long time. It was a good joke, and she enjoyed it. She complained about the slickness of the mattress, and proceeded to lie down anyway preparing for a snooze. Charlotte and I quietly left. It had been great fun, and Annie had given us a wonderful treasure.

The next visit she seemed much more herself. She acknowledged this, saying, "Oh yes, and I was painting in my dream, and it seemed so real."

"I wish I could have seen it too," I responded, hoping to hear some details.

"Yes, it was back home, and George was in it...a visit, I think, and I will remember it. A lot of flowers were in bloom. I love the flowers."

"Well, it must have been spring, or maybe summer. How did the brush feel in your hand?"

"Oh, it was a special day."

Knee Replacement, Kendal Style
Janet Spencer

Darn! I'm not ready to become a sedentary old lady! I want to walk well again, like those folks I see from our window striding on the promenade all around the Kendal campus. What I wouldn't give to regain the ability to walk Kerri, our border collie mix, up and down hills on uneven ground through the woods, and to be able to walk to the Center without hurting and limping, and to carry on the various activities with which I have become involved since moving to Kendal four years ago at age 75. I can feel, as the days go by, and as my physical activity drops off, that I am becoming more and more out of condition, and I don't like it. It makes me crazy! These were my thoughts leading up to the solution to the problem: a knee replacement.

Having had a complete preview of the process two weeks earlier, on Monday, January 21, 2012, Doug and I reported to Admissions at Chester County Hospital by 6:30 a.m. to be admitted for an 8:00 procedure. Most everything happened as reviewed in our pre-operative session. Next thing I knew I woke up in a bed in the orthopedic recovery area, where I would stay from Monday until returning to Kendal, in Westmorland, on Thursday. I was groggy from anesthesia and pain medication, and immobilized by an I.V. and by a pulsing squeezing machine insuring circulation on the foot of the affected leg. My orthopedist showed up almost right away and announced "There is no reason you cannot walk on that leg. Get up and keep moving." I thought he was crazy, but very shortly he was proven correct as the nurse got me detached from the various gadgets, supplied me with a walker, and got me walking down the hall! Didn't feel wonderful, but it was possible. I tried to surpass the goals set for me, and could usually do so. Best of all, I was already on my feet.

During the three days in Chester County the nurses made sure to keep the pain level controlled, and a physical therapist showed up every day to get me walking farther and farther down the hall. Since no unexpected problems arose, on Thursday a car was engaged to take me home to Kendal, one that could transport me in a wheel chair, sitting up. I was "packaged" in the chair, stowed in the special car that had hooks on the floor to secure the chair, and shipped to Westmorland where a room awaited me with my name on it. How lovely to be back among people I knew and who knew me. There were flowers, too, on the dresser, from some Kendal friends. They could never know how special this made me feel.

My room in Westmorland had a huge window looking out on a courtyard with gardens. In January there were no flowers, but there was blue sky and there was sunlight, and there were birds! Birds were the most comforting feature. Most rooms in Westmorland have a bird feeder outside the window, and I learned how important this connection with nature and the real world can be. The birds were my pets and companions that visited at reliable hours every day.

On Friday, my first whole day at Westmorland, I was wheeled to physical therapy, right there in the same building complex, and the program was begun toward the goal of returning the replaced knee to fairly normal extension and flexion. Unfortunately, I was unalterably connected to that knee, so I had to experience the discomfort it experienced with the program. Chris, my physical therapist, said to be sure to take my pain meds an hour before therapy, and that helped. But I really didn't know how I was going to get through these hour-long sessions three times a week for six weeks. I knew the process was necessary for full use of the knee in the future, and I was very glad to be at Kendal for therapy instead of an outside rehab facility, but no cheery reasoning seemed able to make me look forward to physical therapy. The saving grace was how competent and empathetic the two therapists were, always clearly working toward a goal, and always ready to exchange a little banter to lighten the load. The heat treatment before putting stress on the new joint, and the icing afterward, were most welcome.

At the same time, on day one at Westmorland, the Kendal occupational therapist, came to my room. She asked how I liked the arrangement of the furniture. When I allowed that the bed was not under the wall lighting, she moved everything around herself to my satisfaction! That was the first accommodation to my needs of the many she was to manage. That day she brought a gadget to help put on shoes and socks—which I didn't require. She asked about the comfort of the bed, and had a special soft mattress installed. She also wheeled me to physical therapy many times until I could walk that far (400 steps?). I could walk myself within about ten days, as I remember.

But the bulk of my time was spent in my room, being attended by the staff of nurses and aides. There was no limit on their concern for my comfort and well-being. For instance, the first night, because of pain medication that interfered with sleep, I was lying awake. At about 2:00 a.m. I rang for a cup of tea and a pain pill. No problem. The tea was brought, along with snacks, and the pain med was delivered once the prescribed 6 hours between pills was elapsed. And the tea came with an extended middle of the night chat session about horses, my favorite subject, since horses had largely been my life in retirement before coming to Kendal. That personal attention during that difficult night no doubt healed knee and psyche together.

There was a problem finding pain meds that were adequate and did not have undesirable side effects. My Kendal doctor, a gerontologist was right there to suggest an alternate to the medicine prescribed in the hospital. The Kendal pharmacy procured the new medicine, and my doctor volunteered that I should call him directly at any time if I developed a concern. He said he would much rather take the call right away than have calls pile up. Wow, I was really grateful.

With the Kendal system of informed caring and devotion of staff I made very good progress in recovery. Kendal's geography allows for one-floor access of Westmorland and Cumberland patients to all other areas of shared spaces, such as physical therapy, the coffee shop, the dining room, the library, the auditorium. While I didn't feel like roaming through all these areas, mostly because I thought I looked a fright, friends did drop in to wish me a speedy recovery, and my room ended up full of flowers. I felt all wrapped up in caring.

The occupational therapist's attention to my ability to live safely at home was thorough. She visited our apartment to check out potential hazards and inconveniences. She prescribed a shower chair for me to use in our bathtub. Best of all, she taught me the driving skills needed to use a cart in which I could zip all around the campus to keep up with my usual activities in the community. Kendal actually provides carts for this kind of temporary use, free of charge. After being issued the cart, she came with us to our car to make sure I could get in and out of it successfully.

Nine days after entering Westmorland I was discharged to our apartment. I used the borrowed cart for another five weeks, so about seven weeks after the operation I could manage a normal life, with lots of support from Doug.

Meanwhile, physical therapy gradually became less onerous, and three times a week morphed into twice a week, a much more bearable load. Always the goals were increases in the flexion, in extension, in strength, and an increase in the distance walked. At about twelve days I could walk myself to and from therapy with a walker. At one month I could walk easily with just a cane. One month is a land-mark time because that is the date of the first visit to the orthopedist after the operation. I was able to walk confidently into Dr. Simmons' office, and he was pleased with the results of physical therapy and with his handiwork.

The outcome has been wonderful. At six months the knee felt good, but by a year it was even better. Now, after a year and a half, the knee functions normally. No more sleepless nights due to knee pain, no more limping, no more limitations on activity. I happily walk our dog through the woods daily and recently walked through Longwood Gardens on pavement for more than an hour with no adverse effect on my new knee. Sessions in our fitness room have maintained flexibility and increased conditioning. It is grand to have the prospect of continued normal life. The combination of great medical care and the Kendal brand of devotion of staff to the well-being of residents has been something wonderful to experience. Now I can stride out on the promenade just like those folks I envied before the operation.

When I think about this whole replacement experience, how it would have been without this support, I know how lucky we are to be here. Living as we did pre-Kendal in a rural home, no in-house doctor, no in-house pharmacy, no on-site staff, no friends in the same building, no therapy just down the hall, no meal service, no cart to get me around.... Well, it would have been much harder on me and on Doug to have a knee replacement. I would have had to live at a rehab for a week or more where I knew no one, and would have had to travel several times a week to receive physical therapy after that, involving Doug to drive me. No convenient on-premises fitness room or swimming pool, if that were my choice of exercise. No unified community to take responsibility for my recovery. I prefer Kendal-style knee replacement any time.

Our Caring Community
Helen Ford

I lived at Kendal for two years before the onset of my illness; what a great blessing that was! The time was spent in a normal way, getting to know fellow residents, learning the ways of the community, and becoming comfortable in my cottage.

When I received the dreaded diagnosis, cancer, I immediately felt the support and diligence of our medical staff. Nurses helped to educate me and recommended various doctors whom I should see, all the while surrounding me with kindness and loving care. They mentioned to me the name of a Medical Assistance Companion, a new resident, whom they thought would be willing to accompany me as I made my way along unknown paths. Also, once word of my condition circulated around the community, a number of residents offered all the kinds of help they knew I would need. The support of this loving community played a huge part in allowing me to discover "my new normal."

Hesitantly, I made the call to Carol, the recommended companion. Would I feel comfortable with a person unknown to me, when I was feeling so miserable? My apprehension was quickly resolved as I discovered Carol to be an upbeat, happy person who also happened to be a nurse. She seemed to know exactly how to guide me through the trying days of chemotherapy. Sitting in with me during my oncology appointments, she took careful notes on what the doctor said so that I could more easily explain things to my sons who lived at a distance; then while in the treatment room, she would busy herself knitting quietly by my side for two to three hours as the chemicals slowly dripped into the selected vein of the day. Drawing upon her bag of colorful yarn, she began to create sweaters, shawls, hats while I was dozing off and on. When I would waken, there she would be beside me, her fingers flying!

During this long period of exhaustion and nausea, other residents shared a marvelous assortment of thoughtful gifts—a small bunch of hand-picked field flowers in a tiny vase, a poem or two slipped into a get well card, regular hand massages and with them the gift of touch, relaxation, and good conversation, personally made cards with special messages, and convivial visits helping to make me continually feel part of the community.

The intellectual gifts were amazing! Stimulating conversations kept my brain ambitious and alert. One resident went to the library and found books that she thought might interest me. Another shared her British magazines so that I could indulge in a different culture. Very special was a bouquet of glorious gladiolus raised right here in a Kendal garden. And there was a woolen prayer shawl to warm my shoulders or legs. Then food, averse to it as I was, consisted of well-intentioned gifts of specially prepared simple lunches and delicious homemade soups, mild enough to eat at this queasy time. These presented on very pretty dishes or on a uniquely interesting tray.

Quietly, my neighbor Priscilla accomplished the repetitive task of food shopping. I greatly benefited from a volunteer's trips to the post office, for I needed many stamps for my house-bound volume of correspondence. While many notes of support came from Kendal residents to my open box, I also wanted to write responses to the notes and calls from members of my family and friends from far away.

Then when I was strong enough for a slow walk on the path around the glorious red maple in front of my cottage, a friend or two accompanied me, providing good companionship. Never once did I feel "stuck" in my cottage or lonely. Perhaps I drew upon an early experience when in 1945 I was stricken with paralytic polio. Then, as an eleven year old child bed-ridden for four months, my mother administered Sister Kenny hot packs. They, along with the twice-a-week visits of a physical therapist, were meant to help my stiffened, painful muscles. As a few nerve sprouts grew and attached themselves to the deadened leg muscles, some of these muscles were able to be retrained. Importantly, I learned how to live a distinctive creative life. For this I am so grateful!

Journeying along the cancer trail, like polio, was over-whelming, at times bringing deep discouragement and tears. At other times I felt worn out or tired of all I was experiencing! If visiting with a friend, we would respectfully share these private moments with acceptance.

Being able to remain in my cottage home while under-going the six months of weekly chemotherapy treatment was very positive for me! I loved the visits of Chris, our Kendal nurse practitioner. I well remember the day she visited when I was sitting up sewing instead of being supine. Not only that, but I mentioned proudly to her that I had made my bed earlier in the day! How good it felt to do a simple daily task again, pulling up the sheets and blankets tightly, smoothing out the wrinkles, pleasuring in the beauty of an especially colorful April Cornell-patterned bedspread during the day as I en-tered and exited the bedroom. Much better than pulling up a bundle of disarrayed bed covers at 8 p.m. as I readied my exhausted self for a good night's sleep. Similarly, I was also protective of my desire to wash my own dishes, even though piled high from a few days before. When inspired, I found that putting my cold, tingling fingers, newly affected by neuropathy from chemotherapy, into the warm dish water, sloshing the sponge over the dishes, and placing them after a hot rinse into the drying rack, was a pleasurable reward in itself!

Meeting with the interns whom Chris occasionally brought along on her visits proved intriguing, as these young women were eager to observe how I was dealing with the physical and mental aspects of my prolonged illness. Surprised to realize that I had become a mentor along with Chris, I shared my fears and hopes from the vantage point of being mid-stream in my treatment. I puzzled at length about the medical pros and cons of major surgery. Empathetically they listened to me as I was trying to figure out whether to go for surgery as a next step. The decision had to be totally mine, and that in itself made me quite apprehensive! I'm guessing the young women picked up some interesting psychological insights into my dilemma during these low key late afternoon visits!

As the weeks rolled along, I became stronger and began to get out and about in an electric cart loaned to me by Kendal. I looked forward to brief conversations in the halls with residents and happily received their enthusiastic encouragement. The whole community seemed to be cheering me on! Very slowly my blood was beginning to build up making me feel much better, and hair began to grow back on my head giving me a more natural appearance. Instead of chemicals, the vibrancy of life was surging through my veins!

Then it came time for me to get down to the nuts and bolts of a surgical decision. What path was I going to follow for my ovarian cancer, stage III? It was my call. Surgery was the recommended treatment with the best known outcome for younger women in similar circumstances. After an interview with the surgeon at HUP in Philadelphia, it seemed the natural thing to do, seeing that I could combine this surgery with another surgery which needed to be done. I signed the necessary papers without hesitation, but didn't fully realize the extent of my commitment until weeks later!

There was no time to worry or stew about the decision made since I immediately became caught up in a flurry of activity to make myself as strong as possible for the surgery. Pushing and pulling elastic bands with both arms and legs, as well as time on the NuStep, and brisk distance walking were a few of the challenges. All of this was accomplished right here in the Physical and Occupational Therapy Department where we worked together to strengthen my entire body, but especially my weakened leg muscle left from the onslaught of polio almost 70 years before.

Gradually the days ticked by, and with the support of

the medical staff, bolstered by the good wishes of many residents and friends, I faced major surgery, actually three procedures rolled up into one.

Not knowing how my 79-year-old body would react to this tremendous stress, but trusting in the skills of my surgeons, buoyed and upheld by the power of prayer, as well as being Held in the Light by my Quaker friends, I stepped forward, almost as if walking on water. No time for second thoughts or fear when the head surgeon stopped by my hospital bed, greeted me with a broad smile, and told me that I was next in line for surgery that afternoon of February 28, 2014.

Fortunately, all went very well, and the surgeries moved along more quickly than anticipated. The chemotherapy had done a spectacular job! For a handful of days I recovered in this busy, noisy teaching hospital, and then returned to Kendal. What pleasure I experienced while being pushed on a gurney down the halls of the Westmorland nursing area, towards a quiet wallpapered room near the end of a hall. Ah, its feeling was subdued and restful. I was "home" and very comfortable, taken care of by an efficient, well trained medical staff. My sons need not worry about my care. Along with delicious food which I selected from a menu each day, occupational and physical therapy kept me busy, pushing me almost to the point of exhaustion. When it was determined that I was strong enough and physically able to handle living in my residence, I was moved back home to my cottage by the staff and settled in with their help. Evening meals were delivered to me there until it became time for me to join other residents in the dining room for social interaction. Kendal had seamlessly eased my way to recovery!

And so, with my cancer in remission and with the continuation of good "all around care" provided by Kendal, I am experiencing new life! Present treatment ended symbolically a few days before Easter with the completion of five sessions of brachytherapy (radiation.) Thanks be to God, I was able to celebrate a milestone birthday and step into the new elder stage of life to be enjoyed fully at Kendal with friends and staff!

Neva, It's You!
Neva Riviere

"Millie, this is Neva, a volunteer, who has come to play Scrabble with you. Would you like that?"

I looked into the eyes of a petite woman, bent over, sitting in an awkward position in a wheel chair that seemed too large for her small frame.

"That would be very nice," she replied in a quiet voice that did not have a very convincing ring to it.

I had been told that Millie had recently been moved to a new room and was anxious, confused and in need of constant reassurance. And thus began an exciting journey that has developed into a warm friendship which is mutually satisfying.

Although I put on a confident front, I, too, was anxious, confused and in need of reassurance. I was a newcomer to Kendal, had only worked with youth and did not feel confident about my role relating to a person with cognitive issues. What in the world could I do for this troubled soul?

We went into a sun-filled room with colorful birds in a large cage. It was easy to begin a conversation about the birds while I got out the Scrabble board. Once the board was set up it was clear that Millie was skilled with the game, and she began to comment about strategy, making suggestions about better use of my tiles. This became a weekly visit and both of us were more comfortable, so much so that I suggested we play with a group that met on Friday evenings. Millie agreed.

Unfortunately, for the first few Fridays as we left her hall she had an urgent need to go to the bathroom. Back to the nurse's desk where she was told: "Millie, you just went to the bathroom. You don't need to go again." Nevertheless, the staff complied with her request. We dealt with this issue by having the staff see that she went to the bathroom just before I came for her.

As time passed she was ready and waiting for me on Friday nights and she welcomed the opportunity to see friends that she had known before she was in the skilled nursing unit. Everyone remembered that she was a whiz at Scrabble, and for months this became a regular event. Unfortunately, it became clear to everyone that Millie was experiencing more stress than pleasure in her effort to keep up. So, she bowed out of the group games.

"Shall I pick you up at three on Wednesdays?"

"Oh, no, I don't know what I might be doing and I don't want to have you come all this way and me not be able to go out. Besides I can't remember things and my daughter may be coming. I don't want to bother you."

We solved this problem by agreeing that I would stop in when I was free and if she had other things to do, that would be fine. I could easily come at another time and if I were busy and didn't show up, then she would not worry. That relieved her mind and the fear of 'bothering' me.

By this time we had established a rapport and I was feeling more comfortable, as was she. The light had come back into her eyes, she was smiling and had begun to exhibit a sense of humor. She was always glad to see me and we had many fine walks down the hall at the Center viewing the art that was on display or the varied flower arrangements that changed each week. There were still moments of anxiety:

"I don't know my room number, how will I get back?" to which I would reassure her that I was taking her to her room, she need not worry. While being transported she would often ask: "Neva, are you there?" As I answered, I became aware of how vulnerable one must feel being pushed from behind.

As the weeks became months, and the months a year the bond between Millie and me became stronger and we could relate easily and enjoyably. I would sometimes drop by for a visit, move her over to one corner by a window and we would enjoy the flowers, the butterflies and the birds at the feeder. She would ask about my family—I took pictures in for her to see, and she would tell me about her daughters whom I got to meet several times. I was sometimes stopped by staff to say that they saw a great improvement in Millie's demeanor after she spent time with me.

One day I stopped in and found the Day Room almost empty but with the film *The Sound of Music* just beginning to be shown. She seemed delighted with the music and when I ask if she would rather watch than go out she answered in the affirmative. We sat together singing the songs that we knew, she commenting on the dresses that Maria had made the children or the actions of the various family members.

During the winter there was a coffee hour following dinner. It was held in the main lounge in front of a fire, with refreshments available. People gathered and visited informally. As always, I explained to Millie the nature of the gathering, the time we might be there. She was eager to go, and once there she met friends that she had known from before she moved to the skilled nursing unit. She was warmly greeted and became engaged in conversations, one with another resident about their common family origins and another, Bill, whose wife had died recently. Millie called his attention to the fact that his wife had had very precise ideas about the proper way to wear her clothes. "Bill, I have always wondered what it must have been like to be married to such a strong woman." There was laughter but Bill had a very appropriate response much to Millie's pleasure, her eyes twinkling.

On one such night I asked if she might be tired and want to go back to her room. Her reply: "Oh, no, it is so good to be with people who are talking." A light bulb went off in my head: she was confined to a wheel chair, spending much of her time after activities, in a room with people who were non-verbal. She could not discuss the book that she was reading or the article from the science magazine that she excitedly told me about. I was learning so much.

We went to the summer fair that was held in the court-yard, and we went to concerts. She was thrilled to see and hear the Kendal Chorus in their winter presentation. She had at one time been a part of that group. I would usually drop by to ask her if she wished to attend one of these activities later that evening. She was always ready to go and there were no longer any bathroom issues or anxieties about what she was to do. She responded to one person, "As long as I am with Neva I know she takes care of things."

People who have known Millie over the years have commented to me that she is like a different person, that I have really done a good job. My response is that I have tried to be a good friend to Millie and that she has become a good friend to me. She is not a 'different person' but rather the same person who has had one-on-one attention from a friend not a health care provider. For me I look forward to walking in, tapping her on the shoulder and hearing her say: "Neva, it's you! How wonderful to see you," as she breaks out into a smile and grasps my hand.

We have come a long way and I look forward to continuing this journey together.

George

Dana Davis Houghton

Coming to Kendal I found much more companionship, on a daily basis, than had been my experience living in my home. It is good to have many friends close by. My need to be alone at times has not been compromised, a concern of mine before we moved.

The timing of our move was precipitated by hints of dementia in my husband, George. We wanted to establish ourselves in a community of friends before the impairments became pronounced, knowing we knew we would eventually need the long term care that Kendal can provide.

George was a very skilled man in many ways. Where do the skills go when one can't access them anymore? He expanded our house by two bedrooms and a bath upstairs, and two greatly enlarged rooms downstairs, doing all the work himself. The plans were drawn, additional cellar space dug out, floors laid, two stairways extended, walls erected, plumbing and electricity put in place, then insulation, roofing, and painting. He also built furniture needed for this home, and constructed stage sets for the local community theatre. Yet now, after taking apart a flashlight, he was unable to reassemble it!

George doubled the size of our garage. The floor had a dug-out pit deep enough for a man to stand in and work on the underside of the car in the garage. The walls were up, the roof on, the rolling garage door installed. Attic space above this section of the garage held summer garden equipment, and a large supply of lumber for future building projects and for turning many wooden bowls on the lathe.

Now, it was sometimes difficult to know if the sock goes on first, and then the shoe, or whether it is the other way around. And if he had it figured out on Monday, he still had to figure it out all over again on Tuesday.

George had raised most of the vegetables for his family, freezing and canning the produce for year round use. He raised bees, and harvested the honey. He tapped maple trees, and boiled the sap into maple syrup. Abandoned telephone poles were collected and cut into eight-foot lengths, dropped into 15-inch holes in the garden, then laced together with baling wire and strong twine to support the Dr. Martin pole lima beans. This required a strong back. He pruned trees and shrubs. He cut down trees that were a problem, always planning where the dropped tree should land to avoid damaging the house, garage or plantings; and they always landed precisely where he said they would.

Now, it could be a challenge to cut his meat, or keep cake or ice cream from falling off the plate, or out of the bowl.

George planned vacations, taking his whole family through many national parks, to lakes, mountains, caves, volcanoes and lava flows, petrified forests and Indian ruins, Hoover Dam and sand dunes, camping all the way.

Now, it sometimes took several seconds of thought to know how to place the walker in front of him, with the wheeled edge leading.

He skied downhill and cross-country and canoed white-water rapids. He hiked long mountain trails with a heavy backpack. He joined family and friends in Scottish Country Dancing every other week, and attended the New Years Eve and Spring Balls each year.

Now, with the stiffening of his body from Parkinson's disease, he struggled hard to lift his body out of a lounge chair. Sure footedness on roofs and ladders and steep trails

154

and wet rocks in streams, had been replaced with unsteadiness as he walked.

In his professional life, he was occasionally called on to inspect ship engines, climbing into the valves after the engine cooled down to look for microscopic wear and tear, the scratch marks left by the use of dirty oil, when the engine wasn't properly maintained. He took photographs of the damage to support and accompany his conclusions and written reports.

Now, it was challenging to fasten his belt correctly, as the dementia aspect of Parkinson's increased.

Where do the skills go, when one can't access them anymore? The pockets of memory are still in the brain, but some of the connecting neurons have been eroded, destroyed like collapsed vital bridges, rendering the memories unreachable.

As his dementia increased, he lost access to the skills that defined his life. Walking was increasingly difficult, as was knowing when it was mealtime, or which way to turn to get to the dining room, or where his room was located. It became necessary for him to move from independent living to the personal care unit within Kendal. The staff was both kind and loving in meeting his needs, making him feel welcome, helping him to see it as his home, never treating him as a burden, but rather as a valued member of the community. The same welcome was extended to me. I was welcome to visit him at anytime, and to join him in any of the activities provided. He was also free to join me in any of the dining room options available, or for programs in the auditorium. When I took him to visit family, I was offered assistance getting him in and out of the car.

Then, following surgery, he had to be moved from the personal care unit to the skilled medical nursing wing in Kendal, but the loving, attentive care continued, even as his mental clarity diminished and his ability to walk declined further. He was escorted to the shower, and bathed. Finally unable to feed himself, staff would feed him, with patience and cheerful banter, even though he could not talk.

How hard it was to see the skills of his mind and hands, his physical strength and joy in working slip away! Throughout his illness, he maintained the phenomenal patience and pleasant attitude he had always had, but his persistence in trying to solve difficult problems was increasingly frustrated as he lost mental clarity.

He will be especially remembered for his openness to people, eagerness to be of help, his loving dedication to family and friends, a warm heart, and a sparkling smile that lit up his eyes and face.

Driving with Medicare Marge
Marge Carrigan

Around 1980 I discovered that driving people who can no longer drive is fun, and sometimes stressful. I was on the nursing staff here at Kendal when a resident asked me how he could get to the Wilmington train station. It was only 15 minutes until my shift ended, so I said, "If you wait until 4:30 I will be happy to drive you there." That is how my Kendal resident driving began. It became a central activity for me when I moved into Kendal as a resident myself.

First, there were five ladies who wanted to take a trip to have lunch in a favorite restaurant over in Delaware. Yes, they did this every month. They asked me to join them, of course at my own expense, and sometimes I did.

Next I had a gentleman who had a regular appointment in Philadelphia. He traveled by train, so I drove him to the station in Media in the morning and picked him up there at 5:00. He was so pleasantly relaxed for the return trip to Media, that several times he slept through Media and had to get off at the next stop, the end of the line, in Elwyn. Then he would get the return train to Media and find me still waiting for him. I learned to take a book along on those days!

Another time, I took a resident to lunch. He expected to be in the restaurant about two hours, so I came home, planning to return to pick him up when the time came. At home I walked out to the laundry facility to do some laundry. When I got back to my apartment I found the answering machine blinking at me. It said, "I'm the bartender here and someone is waiting to be picked up." I was flabbergasted that I had forgotten. Maybe I was getting old? When I got back to the restaurant I found him there no worse for wear, happy enough for all that time waiting at the bar. Maybe, after all, it was a blessing that this all happened before most of us were carrying cell phones. The years have gone by, and there came a time when I would need a driver, and perhaps, even a caring bartender.

But how wonderful life was through all of those years when I was ready and able to drive people who could no longer drive themselves. Trips to Philadelphia and even the Newark Airport, half-day or longer trips. I loved getting to know people, to hear their stories, to learn about their families. Once when I drove a couple to their place in the Poconos they invited me to stay with them for the weekend. I had a wonderful little vacation, as I did again, for a full week, when I drove a resident to Cape May. We had a great time together. I especially remember our pleasure in getting there via the Cape May Ferry.

I have known this community for forty years, inside and out, first as an employee and now for several decades as a resident able to keep on enjoying the people I was once privileged to drive.

Thirty-two Inches of Snow: Rich to the Rescue

Ed Brubaker

We had moved from Kansas and were happily ensconced in our new home at Kendal when we were blanketed with a record thirty-two inches of snow. This is a lot of snow for the Philadelphia area and they aren't sure what to do with it! I awoke that morning to discover not only the snow, but my left eye closed with a strange skin infection running from my eye up into my hair. Although the walks had not yet been cleared owing to the ridiculous amount of snow, Dorie and I waded through it up to Resident Care in the Center.

The nurse soon diagnosed my ailment as shingles, and it was confirmed by Dr. Sitkoff after the symptoms were described to him on the phone. He advised that there was a new medicine on the market for shingles which, if taken as soon as the disease is detected, would clear it up in two weeks. Often people have suffered with shingles for months or even years. Wonderful!

But the roads were almost impassable. Nearly all the stores were closed. Even if a pharmacy could be found open, would it have the new medicine and who could get there?

If you knew him, you'd guess that it would be Rich Lysle. Rich was already a Kendal phenomenon. He'd started years before as a pot washer, worked his way up to Medical Director and later would be Kendal's popular CEO. Then he became famous when, as CEO, he joined the maintenance crew at six in the morning to shovel walks during another storm.

But now, after endless phoning, he discovered a pharmacy down in the New Garden area, six miles away. It had the prescribed medicine, but they'd be closing in twenty-five minutes. Did that deter Rich? Of course not. He found a four-wheel-drive jeep, braved the icy roads, purchased the medicine and delivered it to our front door that day. In two weeks, my shingles was gone.

The Heart Has No Wrinkles
Rosalind Campbell

Some years ago my husband, Dudley, and I attended a workshop titled "Sexuality in the 21st Century: Issues in Later Life," facilitated by two residents at Kendal. One of the features was an Australian film, *The Heart Has No Wrinkles*, about a nursing home that respected the rights of older residents to have private time together.

When Dudley's Parkinson's reached the stage where I could no longer care for him in our cottage, he was moved to Westmorland. I joined him at breakfast each day, bringing along the newspaper. We watched sports and news on TV, I pushed his wheelchair to the coffee shop where we ate dinner with friends, and we often attended evening programs. I said good-night to him at bedtime. But we missed our naps together—not really possible in the single hospital bed.

At an early Care Conference, held every three months,

attended by a number of his caregivers, I remembered that film we had seen and asked whether there was somewhere we could nap together. A short discussion followed, and a few days later the head nurse assured me that a double bed had been ordered for Dudley's room! Soon it was in place, and an eight-by-eleven bright orange DO NOT DISTURB laminated sign was provided to hang on our closed door. How much those afternoon times together meant to us!

One day one of our friends passed me in the hall and said, with a smile, that he had seen our sign. I just smiled in return.

Seko Visits Westmorland
Peggy Gwynn

One of the many reasons I chose Kendal was because we could bring our pets. Mine is a white, furry, friendly American Eskimo dog, Seko, one of the Inuit words for snow. Recently I stayed at Bryn Mawr Rehab following knee replacement and enjoyed a golden retriever who visited patients as part of therapy. I wondered, "Could I take Seko to visit residents in Westmorland, our skilled nursing section?"

"Yes!" said Jan Clodius, Activities Director, who already was introducing small animals, caged birds, and fish to residents.

Our first visit was such a success that I decided to come back on a weekly basis. Seko was friendly even with strangers and, fortunately, obedient. One of our first successes was with a resident who lay perfectly still and unresponsive on her bed until Seko put his paws up and she reached out to stroke him. The nurses were delighted.

Another success was with a woman who rarely talks. After Seko's visit, she began to talk about the dog she had as a child. "It was a little, spotted dog...."

I asked, "What was his name?"

"*Her* name was Spot...of course! She used to... ."

"Oh! What did she do?" I asked.

"She brought newspapers to us...up to the porch." She was still talking when a nurse entered and we had to leave.

Among our most memorable visits were ones with Elizabeth Gray Vining, once tutor to Japan's crown prince. This charming woman long ago had a little white dog, and she called out to Seko and me as we hesitated at her doorway.

Another Westmorland surprise was Jo Mullen, who had studied at New York City's Art Students League. Although blind, she still continued painting. From outside her door I saw her at work, but delayed a visit so as not to interrupt. She told me later that a friend helped her with easels, canvases, palettes. Several of her colorful abstract paintings still hang in Kendal Center. One is signed "Jo" and another, "Mullen."

But my visits were not only a benefit for Westmorland residents, they were a joy for me too, as I got to know the facility and some of its fascinating residents.

A number of visiting dogs appeared, and Seko didn't like it! Was he jealous? Unwilling to share his territory? He barked at them and I ordered, "No, Seko! Stop that!" But he, jealously guarding his turf, would not stop.

Finally, I decided it was time to say "Goodbye, Westmorland!" How lucky I was, for now I know all about our nursing wing and will never feel like a stranger there.

Meditation on a Locust

Peter Schindler

The Locust is a large, 'bug,' easy to see. It just sat there on the hot pavement. I picked it up, (I don't kill bugs or step on ants and I like spiders; snakes too). It came to life a little. The shiny, transparent wings were still but when I put it on nearby leaves it must've seemed safe so it began moving along into the shade.

This locust may not live long but probably a little longer now.

Death always comes to Kendal and we mostly are here to meet it. It's not the hooded, black, scythe carrying specter of legend. Here at Kendal we settle in, live at our remaining best and don't look over our shoulders that much. No, not really. We look around at ourselves, see us in our neighbors and friends and learn, as they do, sooner or later, we will reach out to death, coming near.

Death seems gentle, soothing, no bony hands. The warm hand of the hospice nurse is there. The water pitcher volunteer comes and if invited by gesture or word, sits and smiles, talks a bit and then moves on.

When one of us has embraced death and left with it, we all can know of it quickly, or not. A notice is posted and another one for a memorial service (if agreed to beforehand) and we can go and remember before we move back to our plans and tasks. We know, somewhere, our turn will come.

It's not a war. We do 'fight,' but to enjoy what we have, not to stop the unstoppable.

Kendal is in the GPS that Death carries. We're all punched in. Here we tend to know it in ways that reduce our need to run. We're slower physically anyway. Slow feels OK here at Kendal.

The locust came after 17 years. That time is unlike the time most of us have here on Kendal Island (I call it that). Lots of people talk about the afterlife, heaven and so on. The locust and I find that is where we are.

Remembering is not easy either. Depends, I know, but time nibbles at our memories like a programmed, purposeful bug. It seems to like the recent, ripe ones best too. Older, stale, stable, memories are left for us to stare at and feel again and again (and retell at dinner or lunch).

We store belongings too, like the busy squirrels we see, and like them we can't always find our precious supply. Some of us are the envy of others, having sorted and given, handed over or sold that which clutters closets and shelves. Others approach the needed organization with small bursts of energy, then, feeling the slowness, the couch pulls us and a nap captures the energy, storing the task for later— which is often forgotten.

Death, verifying its destination, checks the sleeper and moves on. The globe spins. The Universe beckons by its vastness and Death has no earthly limits. Death must have helpers, "out there"? Must be.

Interesting.

A Kendal Memorial

Peggy Brick

There it is, a gold-framed notice, "In Memoriam," on the bulletin board next to the reception desk. We gather around, sharing our thoughts, our latest memory of the resident who has just died. Usually we're not surprised. From the beginning, Kendal residents, given our excellent health care, have flummoxed the statisticians and lived longer than we had any right to expect. Most of us, acknowledging our diminishments, move from our precious cottage to Personal Care and finally to the Nursing unit. So, we're not surprised, but we will remember.

It's hard to believe, but in 11 years here, I've read over 300 of those death notices. Many were followed by a memorial service which, without exception, revealed a remarkable life. Little did we know, we who enjoyed this person during their Kendal years, how they were valued by children, grandchildren, friends and colleagues. We reflect and, of course, we wonder, what will they say about me?

I remember Ruth. We sat together in the third row, left, to watch the films, Playreaders, Saturday Night Live and, our favorite, listen to chamber music concerts. As we waited for programs, we chatted about the current selection for our Women's Lives Book Group. Ruth didn't use a computer, so I ordered books for her. As usual, she had paid me before the book arrived, this time before she died. It was Khaled Hosseini's *And the Mountains Echoed,* the powerful story beginning in Kabul and moving a family around the world. Ruth would have loved it. Sadly, now the book is mine.

I'd known about Ruth from Pre-Kendal Memories and her delightful and fun stories for *Women's Ink*, but during the memorial service her grandson revealed Ruth, the Grandmother. With deep appreciation, this young man, her only grandchild, told us about many trips they'd taken to see birds. He described how she'd name them, explain their habits, and encouraged him to appreciate and understand the environment that sustained them. He stood there, tall, competent, grateful. A perfect celebration of a remarkable woman. I wish Ruth could have been here.

Coming Home
Evelyne Bayless

Old friend or new, we meet in pilgrimage
Here on this tree-crowned hill of sun and shade,
Our former years soft-folded on the shelf,
Our memoirs stored in folders in the shed.
We seldom list past honors, children's names,
The triumphs or the tragedies we've known;
The deeper mystery is still ahead.
We try to compass it in different ways:
in sharing books that give our thoughts more room,
in correspondence with a Congressman,
in tending gardens, mindful of our Earth's
green woods and pastures now in jeopardy,
in laughter, like two waves approaching shore
that meet and crest in sudden glad surprise,
in simple acts of service—daily bread—
and in awareness of the gift of life.

Acknowledgements
Peggy & Allan Brick

We are grateful to each resident who wrote a story that gives a unique perspective, a personal glimpse into life at this Continuing Care Retirement Community. We marvel at the variety of experiences shared and celebrate this diversity within our community.

Barbara Parsons, Terry Engeman and Marianne Whitlock, our resident copy-editors, each contributed editing skills and also gave us helpful advice from their many years of experience. Marianne has been an essential part of our editorial team throughout, including much needed technological help. Residents Betty Warner and Norm Ganser gave essential advice and technical skill.

Bill Silbert, Larry Everu and Louise Snyder, Kendal Corporation staff members, gave us vital advice as well as crucial marketing support.

The most amazing contribution arrived the night Fran Nimeck leaned over our dinner table and announced, "I'm a professional book designer, I'd be glad to help." Fran's skill, artistry and devotion to Kendal are evident in the book you now hold in your hands.